# Western Lighthouses

by Bruce Roberts and Ray Jones

SOUTHERN LIGHTHOUSES
*From Chesapeake Bay to the Gulf of Mexico*

NORTHERN LIGHTHOUSES
*New Brunswick to the Jersey Shore*

STEEL SHIPS AND IRON MEN
*A Tribute to World War II Fighting Ships
and the Men Who Served on Them*

AMERICAN COUNTRY STORES

# WESTERN LIGHTHOUSES

## Olympic Peninsula to San Diego

*Photographs by Bruce Roberts*
*Text by Ray Jones*

A Voyager Book

The
Globe
Pequot
Press

OLD SAYBROOK, CONNECTICUT

**Library of Congress Cataloging-in-Publication Data**
Roberts, Bruce, 1930–
    Western lighthouses : Olympic Peninsula to San Diego / photographs by Bruce Roberts; text by Ray Jones. — 1st ed.
        p.   cm.
    "A Voyager book."
    Includes bibliographical references.
    ISBN 1-56440-133-2
    1. Lighthouses—Pacific Coast (U.S.) I. Jones, Ray, 1948– .
II. Title.
VK1024.P3R63  1993
387.1'55—dc20                                                    92-32521
                                                                     CIP


Cover photographs: front, East Brother Light, San Francisco Bay; back, Heceta Head Light, Florence, Oregon
Art by Cheryl Shelton-Roberts
Book design by Nancy Freeborn

Printed and bound in Hong Kong by Everbest Printing Co., Ltd.
First Edition/Fifth Printing

*Ray Jones:* For my mother and father

*Bruce Roberts:* To Cheryl

*Viewed from the lantern room of the Mukilteo Lighthouse (established in 1906), a sleek ferry leaves its mainland terminal and heads for Whidbey Island in Washington. The lighthouse and ferry reflect a navigational partnership almost as old as civilization itself. For thousands of years mariners have depended on shore lights to guide them safely through treacherous waters. Heart of the Mukilteo Lighthouse is its turn-of-the-century lens, designed to cast a concentrated beam of light visible from a dozen miles or more at sea. In spite of its age, the French-made Fresnel lens still does its job as well as, or better than, most "modern" navigational aids.*

# CONTENTS

*A small bulb casts a weak glow down the 115-foot tower of northern California's Point Arena Lighthouse. While many such stairways cling to a tower's interior walls, this particular one is supported by central posts.*

# ACKNOWLEDGMENTS

While working on *Western Lighthouses,* I was referred to Wayne Wheeler, president of the United States Lighthouse Society. His office has the most comprehensive information about lighthouses I have yet found. It made my job of finding the lights and photographing them much easier. His list of lighthouse "photo opportunities" was of particular help to me, as it would be to anyone else with a camera.

Coast Guard Historian Robert M. Browning in Washington, D.C., was most helpful in digging out old photos of long-gone lights and getting copies of old pictures for this book.

An old friend, Jack Weil, came to my aid in supplying old photos of some of the lighthouses when I ran out of time on my trips out West. His photographs add greatly to this book.

I remember in particular the volunteers at Point Arena who answered all my questions and were cheerful even with a cold wind blowing.

At Point Reyes, Park Ranger Jim Kruse opened up the tower so I could get close-ups of the wonderful Fresnel lens; thanks also to the ranger at Point Bonita, whose name I somehow lost.

Cliff and Ruthie made our stay at East Brother Island Lighthouse delightful.

And thanks to the Newport, Oregon, residents who formed the Lincoln County Historical Society to restore the old Yaquina Bay Lighthouse.

—*Bruce Roberts*


Many thanks to Arthur Layton and James Gibbs for their indispensable editorial assistance and to the United States Coast Guard for keeping the lights burning.

—*Ray Jones*

*Pelicans sweep toward the Point Vicente Lighthouse near Los Angeles. As with many Western lighthouses, the land helps this one do its job more effectively. The soaring cliffs give the 67-foot tower a hefty boost, raising the focal plain of its light to a lofty 185 feet and making it visible from ships twenty miles or more out in the Pacific.*

# INTRODUCTION

Long before California became part of the United States, the Spanish lit fires on Point Loma and elsewhere along the coast to call their ships in from the sea. To mark channels and guide supply vessels to the mission and presidio at San Diego, they hung bright candles from poles. Otherwise the king's mariners were forced to navigate the dangerous California coast without the help of lights on the shore. Then came Mexican independence, Santa Anna, and the Mexican War with the United States. By the time the Treaty of Guadalupe Hidalgo ceded California to the United States in 1848, the old Spanish lights had flickered and gone dark.

The ink on the treaty was hardly dry before the discovery of gold in the Sierra foothills turned California from a remote possession into a passion for Americans. Suddenly, the Far West was seen as more than a place where formerly landless easterners carved out hardscrabble homesteads. It had a value that could be counted out in dollars, a lot of them. It offered not only cheap land and plenty of it but also the opportunity to get rich quick. The California gold rush was on.

Thousands of nearly trackless miles of wilderness separated the settled eastern states from the nation's newest and apparently richest seaboard. Obviously, most of the would-be millionaires who wanted to go to California and pan for gold would have to get there by ship. Just as obvious was the need for safe navigation on the West Coast. The nation could never hope to settle and exploit the West without a secure coastline, inviting to seaborne commerce.

## GRAVEYARD OF THE PACIFIC

It had taken hundreds of years for European colonists to populate North America's East Coast. Even at this relatively leisurely pace, the settlement of the East had exacted a heavy toll. Thousands of ships were broken up by hurricanes, driven onto beaches and shattered by gales, or smashed by uncharted sandbars; uncounted thousands of sailors and passengers were drowned. The West was likely to be built up much faster than the East had been, and it was even less friendly to ships and sailors. Its shoreline stretched more than 2,000 rock-strewn miles, from Cape Flattery in the north to San Diego in the south.

Most maritime disasters happen, not on the open sea, but near the coast. For as long as ships have sailed the seas, sailors have paid with their lives when their vessels came too close to the shore. Destruction and death wait where the land meets water. Ships are built to withstand the stresses placed on them by high winds and giant waves, but a collision with rock, reef, or sand is usually fatal.

Unfortunately for many, such deadly encounters between ship and shore are common along the American West Coast. Stony capes jut out into the ocean like knife blades. Massive sea stacks rise up unexpectedly from the waves. Swift-running streams wash mud and gravel out of the mountains to form ship-killing shallows and block off the entrances of the rivers, where sea captains might otherwise find safe harbor from a storm.

The coastline of the American West is a geologically young and highly active continental margin. In some places mountains are rising out of the ocean, while in others they are sinking into it. Faults, volcanoes, and uplifts have raked and clawed these shores, leaving scores of rocky capes and points reaching far out into the sea. Sharp rocks and gravel-strewn sandbars lurk just beneath the waves. All this makes the coast a navigator's nightmare. And the weather compounds the mariner's problems. The prevailing winds and the powerful gales that sometimes accompany them blow out of the Pacific, driving vessels toward, not away from, the coast with its ship-killing rocks.

In the East, Cape Hatteras won dubious distinction as "the graveyard of the Atlantic." But the West has no maritime hazard comparable to Hatteras—at least none that stands out from the others. All of the West Coast is dangerous. All of it is a graveyard for ships and sailors.

## LIGHTING THE WEST

To help mariners navigate safely in the face of these dangers, Congress launched an ambitious construction program aimed at raising lighthouse towers at strategic locations all along the West Coast. Generally speaking, lighthouses perform two key services: They help pilots and navigators keep their ships on course, and they warn of impending calamity. The latter is, of course, their most vital and dramatic function. Lighthouses save ships, and they save lives.

With this in mind, government lighthouse officials hurried a survey team to the West in 1848. For months its members painstakingly navigated the wild and dangerous western shores. On more than one occasion the survey ships themselves came near disaster for lack of adequate charts and shore lights to guide their pilots. But the surveyors persevered, approaching treachous headlands, sizing up dangerous rocks, sounding river channels, charting capes and points, noting likely construction sites, and even meeting with local Indian chiefs, perhaps to see if their tribes were hostile and likely to attack construction crews.

Before long the team had compiled a report recommending the establishment of a string of lighthouses

*Seen here from California's scenic Highway 1, Point Sur Lighthouse flashes its warning—"Keep away!" This lighthouse guards the spectacular Big Sur coast, as dangerous to ships and seamen as it is beautiful.*

*Built in 1854 on San Francisco Bay's Alcatraz Island, this veteran of the Gold Rush is the West's first true lighthouse, shown here as it looked during the Civil War. Note the long rows of stacked cannonballs.* **(Courtesy National Archives)**

reaching from Canada to Mexico. The report pointed to locations where the need for coastal markers was most critical—key harbors, important river entrances, threatening rocks and reefs. By 1852 Congress had narrowed down the survey list to sixteen sites where construction of lighthouses was to begin immediately. Included in the congressional authorization were Alcatraz Island, Fort Point, Point Bonita, and the Farallon Islands near San Francisco; Point Loma, Santa Barbara, Point Pinos, and Point Conception along the southern California coast; Humboldt Harbor and Crescent City in northern Calfornia; Cape Disappointment and the entrance of the Umpqua River in Oregon; and Cape Flattery, New Dungeness, Smith Island, and Willapa Bay (Cape Shoalwater) in Washington. Congress appropriated a total of $148,000 to launch the project, an impressive sum at the time, but one that would quickly prove woefully inadequate.

In an attempt to stretch these federal dollars as far as possible, government officials decided to hire a single contractor to build the first eight lights, seven of them in California and one in Oregon. Unfortunately, the savings that might have been realized through this approach never got beyond the door of the U.S. Treasury in Washington, D.C. Through a corrupt paper-shuffling scheme, the contract was let to an unscrupulous Treasury Department official who understood nothing whatsoever about the construction of lighthouses. He had no intention, however, of building them himself. He quickly sold the contract to a Baltimore firm, reaping a handsome profit in the process.

The company that ended up with the contract was a partnership consisting of Francis Kelly and Francis Gibbons. The latter was a veteran lighthouse engineer who had built the Bodie Island Lighthouse on the Outer Banks of North Carolina. With their contract in hand, Kelly and Gibbons loaded up the sailing ship *Oriole* with nails, lumber, and supplies and sent it off to California by way of storm-lashed Cape Horn.

When the *Oriole* arrived at San Francisco late in 1852, Gibbons's construction crew began work immediately on the Alcatraz Island Lighthouse. Gibbons believed he and his men could build several lighthouses at once and that the work could be done faster and more efficiently in stages. So once the foundation was finished on Alcatraz, he moved part of his crew to Fort Point, where they prepared the site and started laying a second foundation. Hopping from place to place in this way, Gibbons's workers had four lighthouses standing within ten months. Then disaster struck.

In August 1853, the *Oriole* set sail from San Francisco to the mouth of the Columbia River, where work was scheduled to begin on a fifth lighthouse at Cape Disappointment. Having no light to guide her, the ship struck shoals near the entrance of the river and began to take on water. Feverish efforts to save the vessel proved unsuccessful, and she sank, carrying all the remaining construction materials down with her. Fortunately, the ship's crew and its complement of lighthouse builders were rescued.

Gibbons and Kelly scrambled frantically to replace the lost materials. Within a few months the partners had commissioned another ship and stocked her with supplies so that work could resume. By redoubling their efforts and working on several sites at once, they were able to get the project back on schedule. In August 1854, one year after the sinking of the *Oriole,* the last brick was laid on the Point Loma Lighthouse. All eight of the contracted lighthouses were now complete.

*Dwarfed by the soaring Golden Gate Bridge, the squat Fort Point Lighthouse stands on the walls of a mid-nineteenth-century brick fortress. An earlier light tower was demolished (before it was ever used) to make room for the fort.* (**Courtesy John W. Weil**)

Ironically, although eight lighthouse towers now stood along the West Coast, only two were able to display a light. The recently established Lighthouse Board in Washington had decided to equip the new lighthouses with advanced Fresnel lenses, which were manufactured in Paris. The prisms of such lenses (many of them survive to this day) were designed to gather every available flicker from a light source and bend it into a horizontal plane. Thus concentrated and directed, the light could often be seen from dozens of miles away. Some of the lenses were also given bull's-eyes, which focused the light and caused it to flash intermittently.

Although a Fresnel lens looks like a single piece of molded glass, it is not. The lens consists of individual prisms—sometimes more than a thousand of them—fitted into a metal frame. This makes them look like giant glass beehives. It also makes them rather delicate.

Fresnels come in a variety of sizes, referred to as "orders." The huge first-order lenses, such as the one that once nearly filled the lantern room of the St. George's Reef Lighthouse, in Northern California, are six feet in diameter and as much as ten feet tall. The smallest lenses, designated sixth order, are only one foot in diameter.

The one drawback of Fresnel-type lenses—and it is a considerable one—is that they require a lot of care. They must be cleaned and polished frequently by hand, and the mechanisms that turn flashing Fresnels are large and cumbersome. As a consequence, the Coast Guard has replaced many of the old Fresnels with airport-type beacons, which are easier to maintain.

On those rare and unfortunate occasions when Fresnel lenses are severely damaged or destroyed by storms or vandalism, they cannot be replaced. The expense

*Oil lamps once provided the light focused by this powerful, first-order bull's-eye lens at Point Arena, California. Today, a pair of electric bulbs does the same. If one burns out, the other shines in its place.*

would be prohibitive, perhaps running into the millions of dollars. The original lenses were hand ground and hand polished by the poorest classes of French laborers, including Parisian children, who worked for pennies a day. It is ironic that the handiwork of these unhappy and unremembered workers is numbered among the most durable and practical devices ever made. No one will ever know how many lives have been saved by Fresnel lenses, how many accidents did not happen because their light was there on the horizon, offering its warning and guidance to sailors. Once completed, these expensive lenses had to be carefully packed and shipped more than 12,000 miles around the tip of South America's Cape Horn to reach California. The West's first Fresnels—a matched pair of third-order lenses—came in the fall of 1853 and were installed in the tower at Alcatraz Island and at Point Pinos near Monterey. By spring, the Alcatraz lens was in place. On June 1, 1854, the keeper lit the lamp inside the sparkling lens and a sheet of light reached out across the dark waters of San Francisco Bay, ushering in a new and safer era of navigation in the West.

Although rightfully proud of their accomplishments, Gibbons and Kelly were in for a shock. So were government inspectors and lighthouse officials. When the next shipment of lenses arrived from Paris, they would not fit in the lanterns atop the

*Very sophisticated for their day, most Fresnel lenses and supporting apparatus were made by the French. The Point Arena lens floats on a pool of mercury held in this tank.*

towers of any of the lighthouses. The lanterns and, in some cases, the towers themselves were too small to accommodate the big prismatic lenses. Every lighthouse had to be renovated, and the towers at Point Conception and on the Farallon Islands had to be torn down and completely rebuilt. Gibbons and Kelly had contracted to build the lighthouses for $15,000 each. The cost of renovations and rebuilding, added to the cost incurred from the tragic loss of the *Oriole,* doubtless more than wiped out any profit the Baltimore businessmen had hoped to reap on the project.

The remaining eight lighthouses authorized by Congress in 1852 were built by other contractors. Most were under construction by the mid-1850s, and the final two, the Willapa Bay and Smith Island lighthouses in Washington, were completed and in operation by October 1858. By that time, sixteen lights shone out toward the sea from their appointed locations along the West Coast.

Many of these first western lighthouses were built following a single basic architectural scheme, that of a Cape Cod–style dwelling with the tower thrusting up through the center of the roof. This design offered the obvious advantage of allowing the keeper to service the light without braving the damp and chilly coastal weather. But the Cape Cod style seemed out of place in the West, especially in California, where Spanish-style architecture was dominant. Later western lighthouses reverted to a more traditional design featuring a conical or octagonal freestanding tower, beside which was constructed an accompanying frame dwelling.

Eventually, as many as sixty major coastal and primary harbor lights guided ships along the nation's western shores (not counting those in Alaska and Hawaii). Not all are still standing, and more than a few have been taken out of service and allowed to go dark. But a surprising number of the old lighthouses have survived, in some cases for more than a century, the ravages of earthquake, wind, and weather. Many of the old lights are still burning, offering guidance to any sailor on the sea. Even today, none but the most foolish mariner would ignore their warnings.

This book tells a part—admittedly a small part—of the story of America's great western lighthouses. Through words and pictures, it gives the reader a look at these unique structures as well as a glimpse at their fascinating histories. Each, as you'll see, has its own rich story to tell. The book can also be used as a guide to the lights. General directions and travel information are provided for each of the nearly fifty lighthouses listed in one of four chapters—"Lights of the Olympic Coast: Washington"; "Lights of the Rocky Shores: Oregon"; "Lights of the Redwood Coast: Northern California"; and "Lights of the Golden Shores: Southern California." Some of the lights, though inaccessible, can still be seen from nearby vantage points, directions to which are also included.

Each chapter opens with a visit to one or more of its region's most dramatic and inaccessible lighthouses. These include major island lights such as Cape Flattery, Southeast Farallon, and Anacapa and rock lights such as Tillamook Rock and St. George Reef. Building them required extraordinary ingenuity, courage, and strength. Servicing them demanded the best their keepers could give—sometimes all they could give and more. Each in its own way is a symbol, the distilled essence of a noble navigational tradition reaching back to the beginnings of civilization.

# CHAPTER ONE

# LIGHTS OF
# THE OLYMPIC COAST

## Washington

*Although lighthouse keepers often faced loneliness and hardship, some perhaps considered their lives idyllic. Surrounded by lush summer growth, a 1940s-era keeper enjoys the company of his wife and family mutt at isolated Cape Flattery Light Station in Washington.* **(Courtesy U.S. Coast Guard)**

# Lights of the Olympic Coast

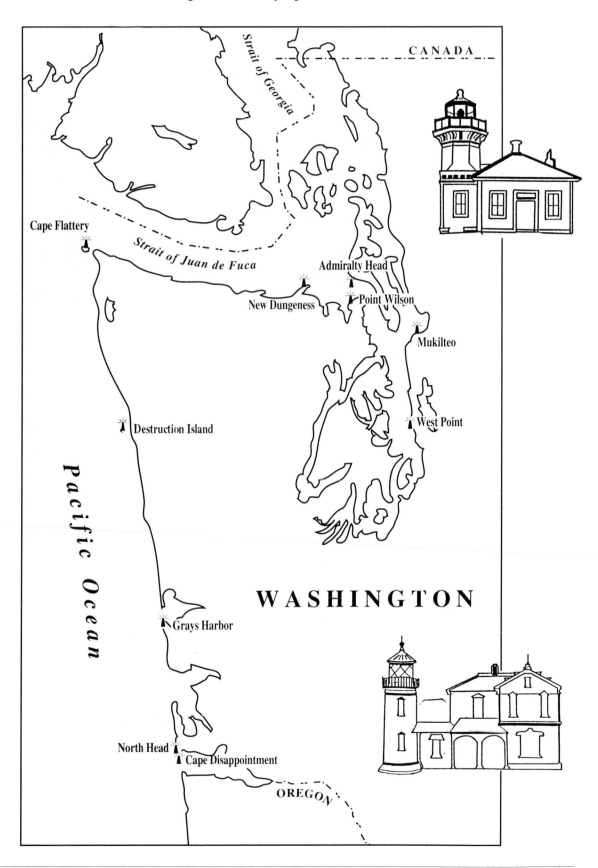

CANADA

*Strait of Georgia*

Cape Flattery

*Strait of Juan de Fuca*

Admiralty Head

New Dungeness

Point Wilson

Mukilteo

Destruction Island

West Point

*Pacific Ocean*

WASHINGTON

Grays Harbor

North Head

Cape Disappointment

*OREGON*

*Located on remote Tatoosh Island, the Cape Flattery Lighthouse marks the lower forty-eight's north-western corner. This 1907 view shows the impressive tower and lantern room—containing a first-order Fresnel lens—rising through the roof of the original lighthouse, a separate dwelling (left), and fog-signal building (right).* **(Courtesy U.S. Coast Guard)**

Just as the northeastern corner of the United States is marked by a lighthouse—West Quoddy Light (see *Northern Lighthouses,* The Globe Pequot Press, 1990)—so too is the northwestern corner (not counting Alaska). The Cape Flattery Light beams out into the Pacific from barren Tatoosh Island at the entrance of the Strait of Juan de Fuca. Thirty miles across the stormy strait is Canada's Vancouver Island.

Not only is Cape Flattery the·most northwesterly lighthouse in the continental United States, it is also one of the nation's most isolated light stations. The sixty-five-foot stone tower and Cape Cod–style dwelling stand as a testament to the loneliness and hardiness of lighthouse keepers and their families.

Among the West's first great navigational sentinels, this lighthouse was completed and placed in operation in 1857, during the administration of President James Buchanan. The stone tower rose directly out of the keeper's dwelling so that he could climb its steps and service the light without braving harsh weather. Tatoosh Island is itself 100 feet high so that the focal plane of the light is 165 feet above the sea.

The original first-order Fresnel lens was manufactured in Paris in 1854. The lens had been purchased for the Point Loma Lighthouse in San Diego but was placed in the Cape Flattery Light instead because the former lighthouse was too small to hold a first-order lens. After nearly a century of service, it was replaced by a fourth-order rotating lens. Its light still marks the cape. A red sector warns mariners of Duncan Rock, a ship-destroying rock that rises unexpectedly out of the turbulent Pacific waters.

A U.S. Signal Corps weather station was established on the island in 1883. Mother Nature gave the hardy weathermen plenty to measure—an average of 215 inches of rain a year and seasonal storms of prodigious ferocity.

## KEEPERS, NOT HERMITS

Nowadays, the Cape Flattery Lighthouse is automated. The mechanisms that control its light receive their instructions electronically, and Coast Guard operators and maintenance personnel need to visit the station only occasionally. But for more than a century, the light was operated manually by keepers who lived and worked at the station. Although their families often lived with them, theirs was a very lonely existence.

Today, of the hundreds of active lighthouses in the United States, only one—the Boston Harbor Lighthouse—has a keeper in residence. So, for all practical purposes, the profession of lighthouse keeper is extinct in America. But it is far from forgotten. Living at the very edge of the sea and maintaining their life-saving sentinels, the keepers and their lighthouses appeal to our romantic instincts.

It might logically be assumed that the keepers, because of their choice of profession, were hermits—lovers of craggy, storm-beaten rocks unpopulated except for birds, lichens, and themselves. Like most simplistic notions, however, this one is false. Generally speaking, people accepted work as lighthouse keepers, not because they were antisocial, but because it was job. It offered them steady employment, certain if moderate pay, and a place to live.

Often, keepers and their families suffered greatly from their isolation, especially at remote stations such as Cape Flattery. Not long before the turn of the century, one Cape Flattery keeper found that he could no longer endure the loneliness of life on his faraway rock. Having decided to put an immediate end to his misery, he attempted suicide by jumping off one of the island's precipitous cliffs. The disconsolate keeper fell nearly a hundred feet onto the wave-swept boulders below, but some miracle preserved his life. Before the tide came up to swallow him, his assistants found him lying unconscious on the rocks. Hoisting him to safety, they carried him back to the keeper's dwelling. Later he was transferred to a hospital on the mainland where he recovered from his ordeals—both physical and psychological.

## THE THUNDERBIRD ISLAND POTLATCH WAR

Vulnerable to gales, blasted frequently by high winds, and under constant assault by the often freezing waters of the Pacific, remote Tatoosh Island could hardly be described as a paradise. Nonetheless, the Indians of Washington's Olympic Peninsula considered it something of a Valhalla. Braving the churning ocean in their dugout canoes, the Makah Indians gathered on Tatoosh—their word for "thunderbird," the native lightning god—to celebrate the summer and, occasionally, to bury their dead. Not surprisingly, they were reluctant to give the island up when officials in faraway Washington, D.C., selected it as an ideal location for a lighthouse.

When members of the West Coast Survey team came ashore on Tatoosh during the early 1850s, they found it occupied by a large band of Makahs who made them feel somewhat less than welcome. Fearing for their lives, the surveyors threw up a stockade and kept armed guards on alert at all times. The Indians were more curious than hostile, however—there was no attack. The Makahs had probably decided that the best defense against these intruders was to ignore them.

In 1853 a second survey team arrived on the island. They unintentionally brought with them a devastating weapon against which the Indians had no defense—smallpox. A raging epidemic killed more than 500 Makahs, over half the tribe. Understandably, the Indians blamed the strange foreign visitors, whom they referred to as "Bostons," for the horrible malady that had overtaken them. They called on neighboring tribes—even some that had been blood enemies—to help them drive off the invaders. Soon, forty war canoes appeared off the island. Disguised as traders, the native warriors hoped to surprise their enemies and annihilate them. The surveyors saw through the ruse, however, and a few cannon shots from the survey steamer *Active* scattered the attackers.

Despite the attack and the prospect of future conflicts with the Makahs, the surveyors chose Tatoosh as a site for one of the first sixteen lighthouses to be built on the nation's Pacific seaboard. Construction got underway in the middle of 1855 and was completed eighteen months later, but not without plenty of trouble from the

Indians. Resorting to a more passive form of harassment, the Makahs stole food, tools, building materials, and even clothing. Eternally curious, they got in the way of construction, and they kept workers in constant fear of being attacked. To hold the Indians at bay, the construction crew built a blockhouse and stocked it with plenty of muskets and gunpowder.

Even after the station went into operation in 1857, relations between the Makahs and lighthouse personnel continued to be strained. The first four keepers resigned their positions because, outnumbered hundreds to one by the local Indians, they naturally feared for their lives. Fortunately, they were wrong about the Makahs' hostile intentions. Given the odds, they would have lost their scalps at any time the Indians wished to take them. But they kept their hair, if not their jobs. The government replaced these reluctant employees with less timid keepers. Luckily for them and for the mariners who now depended on the Cape Flattery Light, their stand on the island did not prove their last.

The bad feelings between the Indians and whites on Tatoosh were to be expected, considering that the two radically different cultures were in collision here. Some of the discord might have been averted, however, had the white men taken time to study the customs of the Northwest Indians. The truth is, the Makahs felt the whites were not only unwanted intruders but quite ill mannered as well. The Indians measured a man's importance not by what he possessed but by how much he was willing to give away. Usually, the giving was done during a potlatch, a party at which the host showers gifts on his guests. The whites never held a potlatch for their new neighbors, so the Makahs thought them stingy, uncouth, and more or less worthless.


## ISLAND OF SORROWS

Although relations with the Makahs on Tatoosh were peaceful most of the time, white visitors had deadly encounters with Indians elsewhere along the Washington coast. In 1775 an expedition of Spanish explorers anchored its ships near where the Destruction Island Lighthouse now stands. A small boatload of seamen went ashore to forage for food and bring back fresh water. Instead they ran into a war party of Indians who made short work of them. In memory of their fallen shipmates, the Spanish named the place Isla de Dolores or Island of Sorrows.

Several years later a party of British foragers received the same fatal reception here. As a result, a nearby river and later the island as well were given the somber name Destruction.

Sometimes the whites in the West were more endangered by their friends than by the Indians. While the Makahs at Cape Flattery never took up arms against the outnumbered keepers, two of the lighthouse men did try to shoot each other. During a breakfast argument, hot coffee was slung across the table and tempers flared. Scalded and red with anger, the two hotheads resolved to fight a duel to the death. In a field beside the light tower, they both emptied their pistols without scoring a hit. By this time heads had cooled, and the gunmen decided that it was possible, after all, for the two of them to live on the island in peace. Only much later did they learn that a friend had loaded their pistols with blanks.

# WEST POINT LIGHT

**Seattle, Washington – 1881**

Accessible

Rising twenty-three feet above a low sandy point at the north entrance to Elliott Bay, West Point Lighthouse has welcomed ships to Seattle for more than 100 years. Situated five miles from the city's thriving urban business core, the old lighthouse stands at the foot of Magnolia Bluff in Seattle's Discovery Park.

The little lighthouse was built in 1881 at a cost to taxpayers of $25,000, a rather princely sum in those days. It was originally fitted with a complex fourth-order Fresnel lens. Manufactured by a veteran lensmaker in Paris, it had twelve bull's-eyes to focus its light and cause it to flash. The light first shined on November 15, 1881, and, according to a Coast Guard estimate, has since put in more than 400,000 hours of nighttime service. Its white beam is visible from fifteen miles away.

*Tiny West Point Lighthouse, located in Seattle's Discovery Park, was among the last lights in the West to be automated. It had a resident keeper until 1985.* **(Courtesy U.S. Coast Guard)**

The station has employed a variety of fog signals, the first of them a bell placed in the tower. Later the station warned ships with a steam whistle and, later still, a Daboll fog signal (named for its inventor), which directed a whistle blast through a large trumpetlike device.

Earlier in this century the lighthouse was a favorite duty station for career coast-guardsman Christian Fritz. The gentle landscape allowed Mrs. Fritz, who was blind, to roam freely on the premises with her Boxer guide dog Cookie. The faithful Boxer clung to the side of his mistress as she cleaned the house or sat weaving, a favorite hobby. While Fritz, a chief boatswain's mate, tended to the light, Mrs. Fritz, Cookie, and the Fritzes' daughter Christy would take long strolls. Unlike the terrain sur-rounding most lighthouses, there were no precipices here to endanger them.

Fritz was not the only coastguardsman who considered West Point an idyllic sta-tion. When the lighthouse had its one hundredth birthday in 1981, keeper Marvin Gerber climbed onto the roof and poured champagne over it. Ironically, Gerber was to be among the light's last keepers. It was automated in 1985.

One of the first keepers was George Fonda, who came to the station in 1883. Fonda became an apparently unwilling model for the Lighthouse Service when it tried out a new uniform on him. Consisting of navy blue trousers, a matching dou-ble-breasted coat with brass buttons, and a billed cap, the uniform was intended to raise the esteem of lighthouse keepers and foster esprit de corps. But for Fonda, wearing the new uniform was a chore. It is said he wore it only when he knew inspectors or important guests were arriving. He must have grumbled and donned the fancy uniform frequently, because the station's guest registery is long and impressive.

People continue to visit the light to this day, but there is no longer a keeper to welcome them. Nonetheless, visitors will find much that is worth seeing. Most of the station's original equipment is on display in the original buildings. Just north of the lighthouse is the Lake Washington Ship Canal and the Hiram M. Chittenden Locks, which link Puget Sound to lakes Union and Washington.

*A popular attraction of Seattle's Discovery Park, the lighthouse is located about 1 1/2 miles from the entrance. Most visitors choose to take the convenient park shuttle bus to the lighthouse grounds. Those who wish to drive should get a parking permit at park headquarters. A pleasant way to enjoy an exterior view of the lighthouse is to take a relaxed stroll along West Point Beach. The park visitors' center is open daily until 5:00 P.M. but is closed on holidays. Park roads are closed to vehicles after 11:00 P.M. each night.*

# MUKILTEO LIGHT
## Mukilteo, Washington – 1906

Accessible

The Mukilteo Lighthouse stands on historic ground. Isaac Stevens, governor of the Washington Territory, signed a treaty here with the northwestern Indians in 1855. The name is an English version of a native American word meaning "good place for camping," and indeed Indians often gathered on this point of land in the days before whites took the land for their own.

*The Mukilteo Lighthouse overlooks Possession Sound in Washington State. The thirty-foot octagonal tower is attached to the fog signal building.*

Early in this century the Lighthouse Board decided to place a light and fog signal on the point to help guide vessels headed for Everett. Completed in 1906, the Victorian-style structure was fitted with a fourth-order Fresnel lens and equipped with a Daboll trumpet to warn ships plowing blindly through fog or heavy weather.

According to visitors, the station's dwelling was quite comfortable and was warmed by steam heat. The first keeper was Peter Christianson, who must have felt very much at home there. He remained on the job until 1925, when he died at the lighthouse of natural causes.

In 1960 the Coast Guard planned to replace the station's Fresnel lens with an airport-type beacon. Residents of Mukilteo and other nearby towns protested, however, and the old Fresnel remains in operation to this day, sending out a flash of white light every five seconds.

*Active since 1906, the Mukilteo Lighthouse contains a Coast Guard photographic exhibit on the lighthouses of Puget Sound. Located in Mukilteo near the landing for the Whidbey Island ferry, the wood-frame structure is open to the public during the afternoon on weekends. For exact hours and other information, call (206) 355–2611.*

# ADMIRALTY HEAD LIGHT
## Whidbey Island, Washington – 1903

Accessible

Built during the months just prior to the Civil War, the ancestor of the Admiralty Head Lighthouse was among the first lighthouses in the West. The frame structure was begun in August 1860 and completed late the following January, only weeks before the guns began to roar at Fort Sumter on the other side of the continent.

Located atop a knob called Red Bluff, the tower rose forty-one feet from base to lantern and had a fourth-order Fresnel lens. The station's fixed white light could be seen from about sixteen miles and welcomed Puget Sound marine traffic into Admiralty Inlet.

William Robertson, a Democrat, was hired as keeper during the last months of the James Buchanan administration. But as soon as Republican Abraham Lincoln had settled into the White House, Robertson found himself without a job.

*Used by the U.S. Army as an officer's residence, the Admiralty Head Lighthouse was abandoned after World War II. Its walls badly discolored in this photograph taken during the 1950s, the old lighthouse looks ready for a wrecking crane. Actually it was about to receive a fresh coat of paint and begin a new life as a historic attraction.* **(Courtesy Washington State Parks and Recreation Commission)**

*The Admiralty Head Lighthouse served ships entering Puget Sound until the 1920s, when it was discontinued. A masonry structure of unusual design, it is now an attraction of Fort Casey Park on Washington's Whidbey Island.* (**Courtesy Washington State Parks and Recreation Commission**)

During the Spanish-American War era, the army decided to build a fort on Red Bluff to protect the entrance to the inlet. To make room for guns and soldiers at newly established Fort Casey, the lighthouse was demolished. A replacement lighthouse, built on Admiralty Head, was ready for duty by 1903.

The brick tower rose only a few feet higher than the attached two-story residence. But the elevation of Admiralty Head placed the focal plane 127 feet above sea level. Focused by the station's original lens, the light could be seen from seventeen miles out into the sound.

The Admiralty Head Lighthouse had an even shorter active life than its predecessor, however. Changes in channels and shipping routes made the station obsolete, and it was discontinued in 1927. Soon the lantern was removed and placed atop the newly renovated New Dungeness Lighthouse. During World War II the lighthouse served as quarters for an officer at the nearby fort. Today the restored lighthouse is a museum and popular tourist attraction.

*The lighthouse is located in Fort Casey State Park near the Keystone-Port Townsend ferry slip a few miles from the historic town of Coupeville on Whidbey Island. The park is open all year during daylight hours, but visitors may tour the lighthouse only during the summer.*

# POINT WILSON LIGHT
## Port Townsend, Washington – 1914

Accessible

It was a sickening sound—the grinding and screeching of one metal ship's hull against another. It is easy to imagine that lighthouse keeper William Thomas winced when he heard it on April 1, 1921. Point Wilson was cloaked that day in a blanket of fog, thick even by Northwest standards, so Thomas had no trouble guessing what had happened: Two vessels lost in the fog had slammed into each other. Thomas immediately set to work organizing a rescue effort.

The rescuers soon discovered a tragedy in the making. The freighter *West Hartland* had collided with the *Governor,* a crowded passenger liner. The *Governor* sank quickly in 600 feet of water, but fast work by rescuers and the liner's crew made an orderly abandonment possible. In all, eight lives were lost, but hundreds might have drowned. The *West Hartland,* her bow stove in all the way to the Number One hatch, was towed to a Seattle dry dock.

At about the time of the *Governor/West Hartland* accident, the last of the West Coast merchant sailing fleet was being destroyed by another sort of accident—a collision with history. The destruction had begun decades earlier, as one by one, steel-hulled and steam-powered freighters replaced the old sailing schooners. The lighthouse at Point Wilson is symbolic of this shift.

Traditionally, sailing ships had approached Port Townsend, Washington, along the eastern shore of Admiralty Inlet. A light established in 1861 on Whidbey Island guided them into port. But steam-powered vessels, with their deeper drafts, favored the inlet's western side. As sail gave way to steam, shippers and citizens of Port Townsend, who hoped to make their city the state's foremost port, lobbied to get a light on the western shore, where traffic was steadily increasing. Eventually, the Lighthouse Board responded and erected a white frame tower on Point Wilson.

On the evening of December 15, 1879, keeper David Littlefield lit the tower's oil lamp for the first time. A fourth-order Fresnel lens focused the light, visible from any point along a sweeping 270 degrees of horizon. Soon, a fog signal was placed in an adjacent building. A twelve-inch steam whistle, it was powered by a wood-burning boiler.

Exactly one year to the day after the station's lamp first burned, the American bark *David Hoadley* ran aground on a beach not far from the lighthouse. A flooding tide lifted *Hoadley's* wooden hull far up on the beach so that, when the tide receded, the bark was left high and dry. The crew was able to climb over the side and walk ashore, barely getting their feet wet. Salvage efforts failed, and the *Hoadley* became a rotting hulk.

A Civil War veteran who had arrived in Port Townsend in 1867, Littlefield served as keeper for only a few years. Having married Maria Hastings, a local women of some social standing, Littlefield became a prominent figure in the town, eventually serving as its mayor.

*At dusk a Fresnel lens outshines the last pink rays of sunlight brightening the walls of Point Wilson Lighthouse in Washington.*

By 1904 high tides such as the one that had doomed the *Hoadley* had eroded much of the beach in front of the lighthouse and soon threatened the tower itself. To save the lighthouse 1,500 tons of rock and rubble were piled up to the east and west of the tower, but even stone could not hold back the sea forever.

A new lighthouse was commissioned and was ready for service by 1914. Constructed of reinforced concrete, the forty-six foot octagonal tower was designed to reduce wind pressure on the building. Now automated, Point Wilson Light is monitored by computer from the Coast Guard Air Station at Port Angeles.

*The Point Wilson lighthouse is located in Fort Worden State Park at the far northeastern corner of the Olympic Peninsula. Take Route 20 to Port Townsend and then follow signs to the park, which is open all year during daylight hours. The lighthouse is open for tours only by special arrangement with the Coast Guard. For information call (206) 457–4401.*

# NEW DUNGENESS LIGHT
## Dungeness, Washington – 1857

Accessible

The lighthouse that stands today near the tip or the eight-mile-long Dungeness Spit is the same one built there in 1857, more than 135 years ago. Nowadays, however, the tower is only about half as tall as it once was. Suffering from age and structural weakness, the original 100-foot tower was in danger of collapsing by the 1920s. Engineers decided the structural problems could be solved by lopping off the top thirty-seven feet of the tower, and that is what was done.

The original tower sported a very unusual color scheme. The top half of the brick tower was painted black, while the bottom was painted white. This arrangement made the tower seem top-heavy when viewed from a distance and no doubt caused more than one sailor to rub his eyes and shake his head before taking a second look. For good measure, the lantern was painted red. When the lighthouse was renovated in 1927, it was given a much more conventional paint job—white from top to bottom.

During its early years the light guided not only ships and fishing vessels but also canoes paddled by Indian warriors prepared to do battle on Dungeness Spit. Traditionally, tribes on opposite sides of the Strait of Juan de Fuca had used the spit as a convenient battleground for settling differences. After the lighthouse was built they continued the practice, but now the place was easier to find. Apparently happy to have a light to guide them to their dark and bloody work, they never molested the keepers—only one another.

The lighthouse and the spit on which it stands took their name from Dungeness Point in England, coincidently famed for its magnificent lighthouse. Like its British namesake, Dungeness Spit is a shipkiller. The list of the vessels wrecked on its sands is nearly endless. Mariners have long referred to it as "Shipwreck Spit."

*New Dungeness Lighthouse is accessible only by boat or by means of a 8-mile hike along highly scenic Dungeness Spit, a protected wildlife area. Take Highway 101 west of Sequim and then turn north, following signs to the wildlife area. The lighthouse can be seen from a distance by taking the Sequim Scenic Loop Road. For information on tours call the Coast Guard at (206) 457–4401.*

*The tower of the New Dungeness Lighthouse, shown here as it looked in 1898, was once 100 feet tall; it was dramatically shortened during the 1920s, however, to repair severe structural weaknesses. The lighthouse stands on a sand spit once used as a battleground by Indians.* **(Courtesy National Archives)**

# DESTRUCTION ISLAND LIGHT
## Near Ruby Beach, Washington – 1891

Observable

Located on one of America's most isolated stretches of coast, the Destruction Island Lighthouse took three years to build. Its enormous first-order Fresnel lens was first illuminated on New Year's Eve 1891, and it has shined ever since.

*Destruction Island Lighthouse is closed to the public but can be seen from a parking area off Highway 101 about a mile south of Ruby Beach.*

*Destruction Island and its lighthouse, seen here from the air, are located just off the western edge of the Olympic Peninsula in Washington.* **(Courtesy U.S. Coast Guard)**

# GRAYS HARBOR LIGHT
### Westport, Washington – 1898

Accessible

Towering more than 100 feet from its base to its lantern, the octagonal Grays Harbor Lighthouse is one of the tallest on the Pacific coast. With its white masonry tower and black lantern, the nearly century-old structure is an architectural masterpiece, a fact not lost on the thousands of photographers who flock here to capture the graceful lighthouse on film.

*Crowned by its glowing lantern room, the octagonal masonry tower of the Grays Harbor Lighthouse stands like an empress above a forest of conifers.*

Situated about midway along the Pacific coast of Washington State, the light-house serves the harbor and the fishing town of Westport. It also serves as a coastal light, guiding ships through a dark stretch between Willapa Bay to the south and the Destruction Island Light to the north.

The third-order Fresnel lens at the top of the tower was made in Paris by the Henry Lapaute Company. It has three bull's-eyes about eight inches in diameter, emitting white and red flashes. The white sector is visible from twenty-three miles away.

Established in 1898, the station was provided with a steam-powered fog siren housed in a separate building. In fog or heavy weather the keeper stoked the boiler's fires. The station now has a diaphone, or two-tone, fog signal as well as a powerful radio beacon.

At least fifty ships have met their end near the entrance to Grays Harbor, an area frequently racked by savage squalls. No one is sure how many fishing boats and other small craft have been fatally trapped here by storms or by the confusion of sandy shallows. Sailors caught in a storm see the Grays Harbor beacon as a signpost pointing the way to safer waters.

*The lighthouse is open very limited hours on summer holiday weekends. It can, however, be viewed anytime from Ocean Avenue in the delightful seaside town of Westport. For information on visits call the Westport Coast Guard Station at (206) 268–0121.*

# NORTH HEAD LIGHT

**Ilwaco, Washington – 1898**

Accessible

For the keeper of the North Head Lighthouse, World War II came very close to home. One night not long after the Japanese surprise attack on Pearl Harbor, an enemy submarine surfaced and opened fire on Fort Stevens, located on the opposite (Oregon) side of the Columbia River. Hearing the boom of the submarine's deck gun, the keeper shut off the light. Likely he stood in the darkened lantern room atop the light tower and watched the bright flashes of the gun and its exploding shells. The raid was brief, and the Japanese did not return.

The North Head Lighthouse has seen a lot of excitement since it was completed in 1898. Built at a cost of $25,000, the station was established to warn ships approaching the Columbia from the north. Mariners complained that they could not see the nearby Cape Disappointment Light from that direction. By the time the new lighthouse was built, the headland's beaches had already taken an impressive toll of ships.

As their vessel plowed through a heavy fog in 1882, the crew of *Harvest Home,* bound for Port Townsend, heard roosters crowing in a nearby barn. That's the only warning they got before the *Harvest Home* slammed into the shore. At low tide the fortunate crewmen were able to walk to safety. Local residents helped salvage most of the cargo of wagons, but the vessel itself was a total loss and was left to rot. The following year the bark *Whistler* suffered a similar fate. Four years later so did the barkentine *Grace Roberts.*

During a fierce gale in 1891, the British ship *Strathblane* ran aground on the sandy peninsula just before daylight. The crew despaired as the vessel began to break up. To save them, the Fort Canby Lifesaving Service team swung into action. With keeper Al Harris in charge, the station crewmen loaded their boats onto a narrow-gauge train and sped to the scene of the wreck.

By midmorning the lifesavers were pushing one of the boats into the heavy surf. Twice the

*The sixty-five-foot tower of the North Head Lighthouse looms above a marker showing its precise latitude and longitude.*

*The impressive North Head Lighthouse guards one of the country's windiest locations. Winds on this peninsula have attained speeds of 150 miles per hour.* **(Courtesy John W. Weil)**

boat was swamped, and finally it overturned. Afraid the boat might never reach them, sailors on the foundering *Strathblane* started jumping overboard to swim ashore. Twenty-four were saved by the lifesaving crew. Two others were pulled to safety by quick-thinking local residents who galloped into the surf on their horses. The struggling sailors grabbed the horse's tails and were dragged out of the sea, alive though a bit humiliated.

The white tower of the North Head Lighthouse is sixty-five feet tall and stands on the edge of a cliff almost 130 feet high. Originally, it was fitted with a first-order Fresnel lens taken from the nearby Cape Disappointment Lighthouse, which in turn received a fourth-order lens. During the 1930s the big, veteran lens was put on display in the cape's interpretive center and again replaced by a much smaller fourth-order lens.

North Head is said to be the third windiest spot in the nation. Winds blast across the peninsula at speeds clocked at up to 150 miles per hour. Trees, chimneys, and fences have been flattened by these gale-force winds. In 1932 a wild duck blown off course and out of control by the wind slammed into the lantern, shattering a window and even chipping prisms in the lens. With the wind in mind, builders fixed handrails to the lantern-room window frames so the keepers could grasp them firmly while cleaning the glass. Legend has it that a keeper's wife, unable to bear the howling of the winds, jumped to her death from the cliff.

Until the light was automated in 1961, keepers entered the tower through a small workroom that was edged with mosaic tile. Today this practical but handsome room still has its original desk and wood-burning stove. The station's two dwellings are now occupied by Fort Canby State Park personnel. When accompanied by guides, visitors are allowed to climb the sixty-nine steps to the top of the tower. The enormous lens that once crowned the tower is a prime attraction at the Lewis and Clark Interpretive Center at Fort Canby State Park.

*From the town of Ilwaco off Highway 101, follow signs to Cape Disappointment and Fort Canby State Park. Markers inside the park point the way to the lighthouse. The nearby Lewis and Clark Interpretive Center is well worth a visit. It is open seven days a week from 9:00 A.M. to 5:00 P.M. May through September and only on weekends during the rest of the year. Fort Canby is open all year long during daylight hours.*

# CAPE DISAPPOINTMENT LIGHT
## Ilwaco, Washington – 1856

Accessible

It was near midnight—the middle of a workday at a lighthouse. Soaked by rain and sea spray and buffeted by high winds, a young third assistant keeper clung to a lightning-rod cable. Lowering himself down the slick side of the fifty-three foot conical masonry tower, he tried desperately to gain reentry.

George Esterbrook, seventeen years old at the time, had stepped onto the tower's catwalk to wipe frost from the lantern panes when the wind blew the access door shut. Try as he might, he could not get it open.

Hanging from the cable, he lowered himself over the edge and, dangling more than fifty feet above the ground, swung himself onto a secondary catwalk below the lantern. Momentarily stunned by the fall, he shook his head and found an unlatched door. Once he was safely inside, the exhaustion of his ordeal caught up with him. He lay in a heap on the watch-room floor until it came time to rewind the light's weight mechanism. Then he went back to work.

Esterbrook later became a physician. It is said he applied the same dedication to the medical profession that he had to being an assistant lighthouse keeper.

Cape Disappointment is a bold headland overlooking the meeting place of the Columbia River and the Pacific Ocean. It was named by fur trader John Meares, who mistook the headland for another landfall and, realizing his error, sailed away in disappointment.

*Many vessels have met destruction on or near this stony cape that bears the name "Disappointment." Poised on top of the cliff, the Cape Disappointment Lighthouse warns mariners of danger. To the right, the Columbia River flows into the Pacific.* (**Courtesy U.S. Coast Guard**)

The captains of many other ships have encountered another, more bitter, form of disappointment at the cape. Countless vessels have foundered here. The Columbia is America's second largest river. It churns the ocean near its entrance, and its bar is particularly treacherous.

The U.S. Coast Survey recommended erecting a lighthouse on the cape as early as 1848, but eight years went by before one was finally built. The oil lamp inside its first-order Fresnel lens was first lit on October 15, 1856, the same year that James Buchanan was elected president of the United States. Construction of the Cape Disappointment Lighthouse proved extraordinarily expensive. It cost $38,500, more than a quarter of the $148,000 appropriation set aside by Congress for the construction of the first nine Pacific Coast lighthouses.

Before the lighthouse marked the cape, settlers had used a white flag in the day and set trees on fire at night to guide mariners. Later they created a day mark by cutting the tops off of trees growing on the headland. Meanwhile, the flow of vessels in and out of the river increased steadily. Most were engaged in hauling lumber or involved in the fur trade with China.

*Completed in 1856, the Cape Disappointment Lighthouse, seen here from above the cliffs, was one of the first lighthouses on the nation's Pacific coast.* (**Courtesy U.S. Coast Guard**)

Completion of the Cape Disappointment lighthouse was delayed by an incident that dramatized its necessity. In the fall of 1853 the bark *Oriole* foundered on the Columbia River bar while attempting to deliver building materials for the tower. No lives were lost, but construction of the tower had to await another shipment. Meanwhile, workers built a trail to the summit of the cape, cleared a site, and prepared ground for a foundation. The notorious raininess of the Northwest hampered construction. Much of the work was done in downpours and in deep mud.

The lighthouse was designed to minimize damage by moisture. Of particular concern was the station's oil lamp, which was brought around Cape Horn in a sailing ship. The lamp had five wicks arranged in a circle with an eighteen-inch diameter, and it consumed 170 gallons of whale oil per month. With each gallon of oil burned, it produced a quart of water vapor. Grooves were placed in the tower's window frames to allow drainage, and eagle-headed gargoyles were placed beneath the roof overhang to drain water that condensed on the ceiling.

A 1,600-pound bronze bell was installed as a fog signal. Unfortunately, dead spots and roaring surf often made the bell impossible to hear, and so it was disconnected. The problem of aiding mariners caught in fog was not solved until well into the twentieth century, when a radio beacon was installed.

Although the light and bell saved many ships from destruction, other vessels were not so fortunate. To reduce the loss of lives in wrecks, keeper Joel Munson, who served at Cape Disappointment from 1865 to 1877, organized a volunteer lifesaving crew. Later the government established a permanent lifesaving station at Fort Canby, whose guns surrounded the lighthouse. (Built in 1864, the fort was a troublesome neighbor. The concussion of its cannons fired in practice often shattered windows and even destroyed the station's original fog-bell house.) The fort's lifesaving team was called into action by the firing of a small cannon near the tower. In 1884 the Fort Canby Lifesavers rescued 175 passengers from the liner *Queen of the Pacific* after she ran aground near Clatsop Beach, Oregon. (The liner was later refloated and returned to service.) Today the Coast Guard Station at Cape Disappointment monitors sea traffic with a battery of sophisticated electronic instruments and continues to rescue mariners in distress.

The Cape Disappointment Light is one of the oldest standing structures in the Pacific Northwest and is the oldest lighthouse in Washington.

---

*From Ilwaco follow signs for Cape Disappointment and Fort Canby State Park. The park is open throughout the year during daylight hours. Markers inside the park direct visitors to the lighthouse. A close-up look requires a brief hike from the parking area. Tours are available on Fridays during the summer. For information on tours call the Lewis and Clark Interpretive Center at (206) 642–3029. The center itself, well worth a visit, is open daily, 9:00 A.M.–5:00 P.M., from May through September and on weekends from October through April.*

---

# CHAPTER TWO

# LIGHTS OF
# THE ROCKY SHORES

## Oregon

*Visitors examine the big, first-order Fresnel lens at northern Oregon's now inactive Cape Meares Lighthouse. Unfortunately, the old lens has been damaged by vandals, and Fresnels are so expensive and intricately constructed that they are considered irreplaceable.*

# Lights of the Rocky Shores

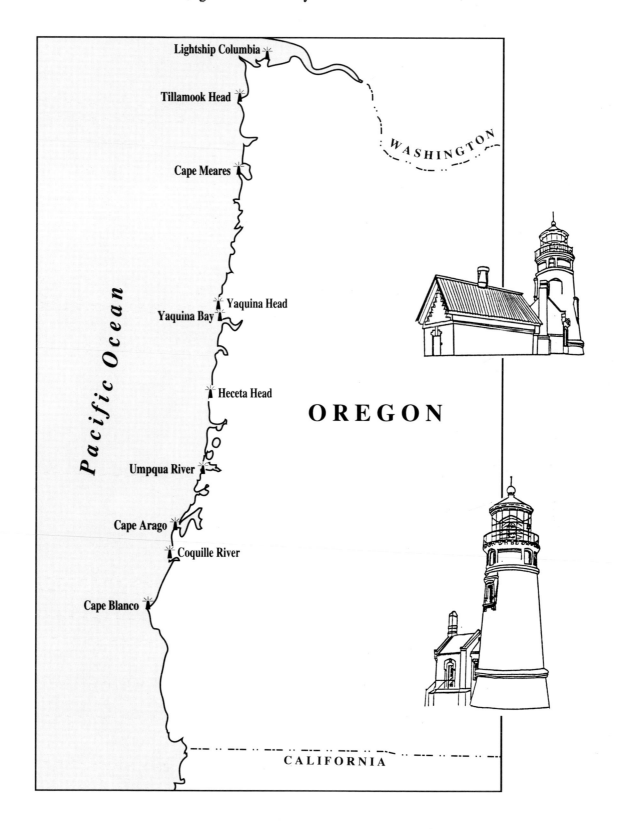

Lightship Columbia

Tillamook Head

Cape Meares

WASHINGTON

*Pacific Ocean*

Yaquina Head

Yaquina Bay

Heceta Head

OREGON

Umpqua River

Cape Arago

Coquille River

Cape Blanco

CALIFORNIA

*Firmly in the grip of the Pacific, Tillamook Rock was probably the most remote and least hospitable light station in America. Its construction was a heroic feat; and keeping the station supplied required fortitude, too. Here supplies are sent across on a cable from a Coast Guard tender.* **(Courtesy U.S. Coast Guard)**

As an outpost of human endeavor, the Tillamook Rock Lighthouse was always as much a symbol as a navigational aid. It marked not only a dangerous maritime hazard but also the precarious and shifting border between human enterprise and the forces of nature.

Located more than a mile offshore near Oregon's magnificent Tillamook Head and about twenty miles south of the Columbia River, this storm-dashed bastion clings to a scrap of rock almost totally in the grip of the sea. In a gale, mountainous waves sweep over the rock and pound the walls of the lighthouse. Few buildings anywhere in the world are so exposed to the whims and power of wind, weather, and the sea. Yet the Tillamook Rock Lighthouse has stood now, more or less intact, for more than a century.

## A TOEHOLD ON THE ROCK

Completed early in 1881, the structure surely ranks among the foremost engineering triumphs of the late nineteenth century. But there were many who said the lighthouse could never be built. In fact, the public took such a skeptical view of the project, there was a general outcry against wasting tax money on so vain and foolish a venture.

Well before the first stone was laid, tragedy threatened to convert public opposition to outrage. A master mason from Portland with previous experience in building seemingly unbuildable lighthouses, John Trewavas was put ashore on the rock one morning in September 1879. Trewavas had been asked to survey the site, but he never even got started. While climbing up the rock's sheer eastern face, he slipped and plunged into the sea. The water immediately closed over him, and he was never seen again.

News of the mason's death raised such a storm of protest that government officials felt they could only proceed with the project in secret. The construction crew chosen for the job was sequestered and housed in an isolated location.

Even some of the workmen—several were tough veterans of other dangerous construction projects—questioned the wisdom of attempting to build on this sea-battered outcropping. The task before them was indeed Olympian. The first two workmen put ashore on the rock became so frightened by the giant waves crashing into it that they jumped into the sea and had to be rescued by lifeline.

Finally, the crew got a foothold when, on October 21, 1879, the revenue cutter *Corwin* landed four workers, along with provisions, blankets, water, and a few tools. These four pioneers were in for a hard time. Soon a gale blew up, driving away the *Corwin* and leaving them marooned. Waves broke completely over the rock, shaking loose huge boulders and terrifying the drenched and generally miserable workers. Over the next few days the *Corwin* made repeated attempts to approach the rock, but the horrible weather always sent the cutter scurrying back for safe harbor in the Columbia River.

At last, more than a week after the first landing, the *Corwin* renewed contact with the rock and its bedraggled inhabitants. But instead of rescuing them, it put ashore five more workers, along with construction superintendent M. A. Ballantyne. Obviously, this job required more than the usual measure of fortitude and determination.

Within a few days the crew had anchored their tools and supplies, built themselves a crude, fortresslike barracks designed to resist the ocean's insistent pounding, and set to work blasting and chiseling a level foundation for the lighthouse. All through the winter and spring the work continued. On more than one occasion gales with hurricane-force winds threatened to blow or wash the little crew off the rock, but they gritted their teeth and held on. And when the winds died down again, they returned to the business of cutting and blasting stone.

By the end of May the rock's pointed crown had been lopped off, making way for the foundation of a lighthouse. On June 17 a lighthouse tender arrived with a load of fine-grained basalt construction stone, and less than a week afterwards, the cornerstone was laid. Six months later the last of the mortar had dried, fixing firmly in place the stones in the combination light tower and dwelling. By New Year's Day 1881 the station's enormous first-order Fresnel lens was being installed meticulously, one delicate prism at a time. Late that day a tremendous gale blew in, bringing the work to a complete, though temporary, halt.

*As this photograph suggests, keepers had to risk their lives to get on and off Tillamook Rock—especially in bad weather.* (**Courtesy National Archives**)

That night workers on the rock began to hear strange noises above the roar of the storm. They thought they heard voices, men calling to them from the darkness. They also heard, quite distinctly, a dog barking. Suddenly, out of the gloom, a large sailing ship came into sight. It reeled and crashed over the waves, obviously out of control. Then, as quickly as it had appeared, the ship was gone.

A day later, when the storm had passed and the sun came out, the fate of the mystery ship and its crew became all too apparent. Its shattered remains littered the rocks of nearby Tillamook Head. The unlucky ship had been the *Lupatia,* bound from Japan to the Columbia River. None of its crew of sixteen lived to tell the story of the destruction. Only the ship's dog survived.

The *Lupatia* calamity provided a somber initiation for the almost-complete Tillamook Rock Lighthouse. No doubt the disaster chilled and depressed the construction crew. After all their struggles they had missed by only a few days having the light ready and shining on the night when it was most needed by the *Lupatia.*

The oil lamp inside the big Fresnel lens was fired up for the first time on January 11, 1881. The light shined almost continuously for the next seventy-six years. It was finally extinguished in September 1957, when the lighthouse was decommissioned and replaced by a buoy.

The lighthouse was never automated and during its active years was always manned. The keepers of the Tillamook Rock Lighthouse lived an isolated and lonely existence, even by the standards of their profession. They were often exposed to the worst insults the ocean could throw at them. On the darkest and stormiest nights, they inevitably grew weary of their rock and questioned their choice of work. Perhaps, to renew their commitment, they sometimes stood in the lantern room and remembered the tragic story of the *Lupatia.* It is easy to imagine that on such occasions, when the wind died down and the foghorn was silent, they could hear a dog barking.

*Supplies are lifted onto Tillamook Rock from the deck of a Coast Guard tender by means of a boom. Calm weather made the process a little easier.* (**Courtesy National Archives**)

# LIGHTSHIP COLUMBIA
## Astoria, Oregon – 1951

Accessible

Among the last of America's lightships, the 128-foot-long *Columbia* was launched in Maine. For nearly three decades, beginning in 1951, she stood on station eight miles off the dangerous Columbia River bar. Retired in 1979, she has since been a prime attraction of the Columbia River Maritime Museum in Astoria.

*Where it was impossible or too costly to build coastal lighthouses, lightships guided mariners. Now on display in Astoria, the lightship* Columbia *marked the treacherous Columbia River bar for more than thirty years.* **(Courtesy John W. Weil)**

*Part of the Columbia River Maritime Museum, the Lightship* Columbia *is moored on the Astoria waterfront at 1792 Marine Drive. Open daily until 5:00 P.M., the museum maintains the lightship as a historic attraction. For museum hours and tour information, call (503) 325–2323.*

*Beached by a ferocious turn-of-the-century storm, an early Columbia River lightship is relaunched. Heavy chains and cables pull the ship toward the water.* **(Courtesy National Archives)**

# CAPE MEARES LIGHT
## Tillamook, Oregon – 1890

Accessible

Like the Yaquina Head Lighthouse well to the south, the old Cape Meares Lighthouse was misplaced by its builders. Government officials had planned to erect the lighthouse on Cape Lookout, but because of a mapmaker's error, it ended up instead at Cape Meares, about ten miles from its intended location. U.S. Coast Survey charts had reversed the names of the two capes. By the time the mistake was noticed late in 1889, the new lighthouse was already under construction.

The confusion and apparent waste of public money stirred considerable shouting and recrimination among bureaucrats and congressmen in Washington, D.C. But President Benjamin Harrison quieted the furor by placing his stamp of approval on the new site.

Completed in 1890, the octagonal iron tower was only thirty-eight feet tall and looked a bit like a squat chessboard rook. It stood on a towering cliff, however, which placed the light 217 feet above the breakers and made it one of the highest navigational aids in America. A huge Henry Lapaute first-order lens, illuminated by a coal-oil lamp, made the light visible from twenty-one miles at sea.

A veteran of three-quarters of a century of service to mariners, the old Cape Meares Lighthouse has been retired. In 1963 an unattractive concrete blockhouse took over its duties. While the new structure is hardly imposing, its 800,000-candle-power light is impressive. It can be seen from twenty-five miles at sea.

The older lighthouse is now a popular tourist attraction. Much to their discredit, vandals have damaged its magnificent lens on more than one occasion. The area around the lighthouse is now a state park and wildlife sanctuary.

---

*The Cape Meares Lighthouse is located in Cape Meares State Park, about 7 miles west of Highway 101 and Tillamook on Three Capes Loop Road. Visitors can park and walk down to the old lighthouse, inactive since 1963. The tower still houses the original first-order lens. Nearby is Cape Meares National Wildlife Refuge.*

---

*Visitors enjoy a keeper's-eye view of the Pacific while inspecting the enormous, first-order Fresnel lens at the now-inactive Cape Meares Lighthouse. Its duties have been taken over by a nearby automated light.*

# YAQUINA HEAD LIGHT
## Newport, Oregon – 1873

Accessible

One of the most beautiful lighthouses in America, the Yaquina Head Light is a magnet for photographers and tourists, who can see it from U.S. 101, the Pacific Coast Highway. The magnificent rock outcropping on which the light station stands is a magnet of a more literal variety. At its core is a rich vein of magnetized iron that raises cain with the compasses of ships passing nearby.

Most vessels sailing up and down the Oregon coast give this headland a wide berth, but not just because it makes their compasses dance. Numerous ships have come to grief along this stretch of coast, many of them within sight of the lighthouse. Some met their ends on the reefs off the headland itself. Long ago, the lighthouse builders carved footholds into the stony cliffs so that shipwrecked sailors could more easily reach assistance at the station. Ironically, two of the wrecks were namesakes—the *Yaquina City* and the *Yaquina Bay,* both lost on the nearby bar within a year of each other in 1887–88.

Completed in 1873, the lighthouse remains in astonishingly good condition, especially considering that little repair work has been done on the structure in more than 100 years. Its masonry tower has conical walls ninety-three feet high, raising the focal plane of the light 162 feet above the sea. The lantern holds an extraordinary twelve-foot-high first-order Fresnel lens that casts a beam visible nineteen miles at sea. It is a fixed lens; the 1,000 watt globe inside flashes at intervals. To extend the reach of its warning, the station broadcasts a radio beacon.

Manufactured by the Barbier and Fenestre Company in Paris in 1868, the lens was shipped around stormy Cape Horn in a sailing schooner. Some parts of the lens inexplicably disappeared during the journey. Perhaps their loss was an omen of the confusing and unhappy events that were to follow. First, the lens and construction materials were landed at the wrong spot, Yaquina Head, rather than their intended destination—Cape Foulweather, several miles to the north. Then the landing itself did not go smoothly. More than one of the boats bringing supplies ashore overturned in the crashing surf, dumping their cargoes into the sea.

Luckily, the lens was not damaged and its missing parts were soon replaced. But by the time the lens was assembled and shining from the top of the tower, it had become apparent to one and all that a lighthouse had not been needed here. Its beacon was redundant with that of the Yaquina Bay Lighthouse. Still, the new lighthouse was obviously superior to its neighbor. The first-order lens of its masonry tower far outshined the fifth-order lens of the wooden Yaquina Bay Lighthouse. So the fate of the older light was sealed and its light extinguished.

*The Yaquina Head Lighthouse fits perfectly into this scene of breathtaking beauty. Its brick tower is a solid piece of work, looking much today as it did 100 years ago when construction crews built it—on the wrong cape. The lighthouse was meant for Cape Foulweather, about four miles to the north. The mistake doomed the nearby Yaquina Bay Light by making it unnecessary.*

*Located off Highway 101 about 4 miles north of Newport, the Yaquina Head Lighthouse is closed to the public except by special arrangement with the Yaquina Bay Coast Guard station at Newport. It can be seen from the highway, the government park, and the nearby beach.*

# YAQUINA BAY LIGHT
## Newport, Oregon – 1871

Accessible

Built of wood instead of brick or stone, like most of its cousins along the Pacific coast, the white-frame Yaquina Bay Lighthouse has nonetheless stood the test of time. Recently restored, it remains today in excellent condition almost one and a quarter centuries after it was commissioned. Its durability is all the more remarkable considering that its light was put out in 1874 after one of history's shortest terms of active service for any lighthouse.

Built on the crest of a hill at the north entrance of Yaquina Bay, it was lighted on November 3, 1871. Less than three years later its lantern went dark, the victim of a bureaucratic bungle. The Lighthouse Board had set aside funds for construction of another lighthouse at Cape Foulweather, well to the north of Yaquina Bay. When the construction materials arrived in the fall of 1872, however, they were mistakenly

*Rendered superfluous by its neighbor on Yaquina Head, the Yaquina Bay Lighthouse was active for only three years (1871–1874). Fortunately for lovers of lighthouse lore and unique architecture, the handsome structure sill stands. Note the small red lantern protruding through the roof.*

*Inside the Yaquina Bay Lighthouse, simple furnishings and an open Bible recall earlier days.*

landed at the headland little more than three miles from the already operating Yaquina Bay Lighthouse. Construction crews quickly rendered the mistake into stone by throwing up a fine tower in only a few months.

By the time the unnecessary Yaquina Head station was complete and ready for use, officials realized that they now had one more lighthouse than was needed to serve the area properly. As a result, the smaller and less powerful Yaquina Bay Light was discontinued. Its whale-oil lamps were extinguished and its fifth-order Fresnel lens winked out on October 1, 1874.

People might have supposed at the time that the abandoned wooden structure would soon be demolished. Not so. The building eventually was put to use as a crew station for the U.S. Lifesaving Service. The hardy surfmen lived in the old lighthouse and used it as a lookout for vessels negotiating the bar.

By the 1940s the weather-beaten building had become dilapidated, and there was talk of razing it. But the Lincoln County Historical Society fought and won the battle to save it. The handsome wooden edifice with its shuttered windows serves today as a tourist attraction and museum. Some believe the building is haunted. Rumor has it that during the 1930s a visitor disappeared without a trace.

*The Yaquina Bay Lighthouse has been inactive for more than a century but is well worth a visit. The Friends of Yaquina Bay Lighthouse and the U.S. Forestry Department maintain the structure as a museum. It is filled with nineteenth-century furnishings and artifacts, including rope beds, kerosene lamps, pewter cutlery, and hand water pumps. The museum is open daily. Its hours are 12:00–5:00 P.M. Memorial Day through September 30 and 12:00–4:00 P.M. the remainder of the year.*

# HECETA HEAD LIGHT
**Florence, Oregon – 1894**

Accessible

In 1775, the year the American Revolution began, Captain Don Bruno de Heceta of the Spanish Royal Navy led an expedition along the largely unknown coast of the Pacific Northwest. An explorer in the service of the king of Spain, Heceta charted scores of craggy outcroppings reaching far out into the sea from the mainland. Heceta was among the first Europeans to look in wonder at the magnificent headland rising sharply out of the sea about eleven miles north of the mouth of the Siuslaw

*With its simple design, stark white walls, and red trim, the delightful Heceta Head Lighthouse shows why some think it the most beautiful lighthouse in the West—or anywhere.* **(Courtesy John W. Weil)**

*Perched on its ocean cliff, the Heceta Head Lighthouse is even more lovely from a distance.*

River. Today that headland bears his name. So, too, does its lighthouse, one of the most beautiful and storied navigational markers in America.

Before 1894 there had been no light to guide ships along the ninety miles between Cape Foulweather and Cape Arago. The crews of ships plying the waters off this stretch of coast were left to find their way in the dark. But in the spring of that year a fifty-six-foot-tall white masonry tower was completed high up on the Heceta Head cliffs, and a bright light began to shine from its lantern.

To build the lighthouse in this remote location had taken nearly two years and $180,000—a fantastic sum at the time. Construction materials had to be brought in by ship and barge to the nearby Siuslaw River and then hauled in mule-drawn wagons to the foot of the headland. Construction stone from the Clackamas River near Oregon City was carried to the site by the lighthouse tender *Columbine*. Bricks and cement were shipped from San Francisco and reloaded onto barges at Florence, to be towed up the Siuslaw by the tugboat *Lillian*. Lumber, most of it from Oregon mills, was unloaded at the river and rafted to a cove below Heceta Head.

The new lighthouse was fitted with an exquisite first-order Fresnel lens supplied by Chance Brothers of London. Its 640 prisms of finely molded glass were as clear as a beaker of spring water.

Light came from five-wick coal-oil lamp. A weighted cable attached to a series of gears turned the lamp, causing the light to flash. The weight reached bottom every four hours and had to be pulled up again by the keeper or one of his two assistants. The chief keeper and his family lived in a house some distance from the tower, while his assistants lived in a second house nearby.

In 1910 the original apparatus was replaced by a gas-type bunsen burner, which in turn was replaced by an electric light. Today, a 1.1 million–candlepower bulb burns in the Heceta Head lantern. The old, but still highly efficient, lens gathers the light and concentrates it into a narrow beam that can be seen from twenty-one miles away. Because of the height of its perch on the Heceta Cliffs, the lighthouse sends its beam seaward from an elevation of 205 feet.

Electric power for the light station is supplied by a local utility company, but the Coast Guard maintains an auxiliary system to keep the light burning in case of outages. During nearly a century of service the light has failed only once, in 1961, when a mud slide temporarily cut electric cables.

---

*One of the most photographed lighthouses on the West Coast, the Heceta Head Light Station stands on a craggy point about eleven miles north of Florence. Although the grounds are open to the public, the lighthouse itself is closed. Some of the best views of the lighthouse can be had from Highway 101 south of Heceta Head, Devils Elbow State Park, and the beach below the head.*

---

# UMPQUA RIVER LIGHT
## Winchester Bay, Oregon – 1894

Observable

The conical, plaster-covered masonry tower of the Umpqua River Lighthouse rises above the treetops of a state park named in its honor. Lush bracken grows beneath the soughing branches. Beyond are acres of sand dunes, golden-hued beaches, and the expanse of Winchester Bay.

At night the flashing light, alternating red and white, can be seen from twenty-one miles away. Coos Bay lies nineteen miles to the south, within range of the beacon. The peaceful setting contrasts sharply with the violent and often tragic history of this stretch of coast.

*As solid as the day it was built, the Umpqua River Lighthouse has stood since 1894. An earlier tower, built in 1857, collapsed after a storm weakened its foundation.*

The original lighthouse was erected in 1857 to mark the entrance of the Umpqua River and warn mariners of a shifting sandbar that had wrecked at least six vessels between 1850 and 1855. The tower was the first of its kind in Oregon.

From the moment they began laying the foundation, the construction crew was pestered by Indians who made repeated attempts, sometimes successful, to steal tools, supplies, and whatever valuables they could lay their hands on. Relations with the local Indians had once been friendly, but they became increasingly strained. Open hostilities were avoided when a construction foreman set off a stick of dynamite. The Indians had never heard such a frightful explosion, and they scattered into the surrounding forests.

Nature provided a more formidable enemy for the lighthouse than the Indians had been for its builders. Only four years after it was completed, the foundation was undercut by floods and surf and the tower collapsed into the river. Despite nearly constant lobbying by Oregon legislators and the shipping industry, Congress refused to appropriate funds for a new lighthouse until well into the 1890s. Eventually, the loss of vessels such as the schooner *Sparrow,* which went down with three crew members at the entrance of the river, forced the government to act.

Completed in 1894, the present sixty-five-foot tower was crowned with a powerful, first-order Fresnel lens. The site, well above the river, raises the focal plane of the light 165 feet above the sea. The flashing light reduced shipping losses, but it often proved no match for the thick fog of the Pacific Northwest. For instance, a pair of coastal freighters, the *Admiral Nicholson* and the *G. C. Lindauer,* came ashore a short distance from the light on the night of May 16, 1924. A pasty fog had enveloped the area that night and blocked the view of the light.

. . .

Not all of those who have moored their lives temporarily or permanently off the coast of Oregon have done so to assist mariners, to fish, or to carry on the commerce of the sea. As with all of the earth's environments, the ocean sometimes attracts evil. On the sea, evil often takes the name of piracy.

One usually thinks of pirates as swashbuckling, eye-patched denizens of the Barbary coast or of the Caribbean during the age of Spanish treasure galleons and the gold doubloon. But there have been pirates in every age and on every shore, even the rocky coast of Oregon.

On the night of August 21, 1909, Oregon's Umpqua River Light could be seen flashing in the distance by the crew of the Alaska Pacific Navigation Company liner *Buckman* as she plied through the ocean about twenty miles offshore. Outward bound from Seattle, she was about to be under siege by a pair of twentieth-century pirates.

The pirates, George Washington Wise and French West, a former sailor, had boarded the vessel in Seattle. Now, shortly before midnight, they stealthily approached the bridge.

Armed with a shotgun and a pistol, the pair had a gruesome plan. They intended to kill the crew, run the vessel aground near the Umpqua River, and then make off with a shipment of gold they believed to be aboard. The ship's passengers would be left to save themselves as best they could.

From the bridge wing the armed pirates burst into the pilothouse. There Wise held the ship's officer and helmsman hostage while his accomplice went aft to rouse Captain Edwin Wood, who was asleep in his cabin. As the ship's startled skipper groped for his revolver in the darkened cabin, West killed him with a shotgun blast.

The shot alarmed Wise, who ran from the pilothouse. No longer facing Wise's cocked pistol, the helmsman hurriedly gave the alarm by repeatedly pulling the ship's whistle cord.

The crew poured onto the deck, and in the ensuing confusion, First Officer Richard Brennan slipped into the captain's cabin. There he found the captain's revolver; he then hurried to the pilothouse, where he wounded West in a shootout. The bloodied pirate leapt over the side into the darkness, never to be seen again.

Later Wise was found cowering below decks. The crew clamped him in irons and, when the ship reached port, turned him over to the authorities. Eventually, he was sent to an asylum for the criminally insane.

The *Buckman* had not been carrying gold that night.

---

*The Umpqua River Lighthouse can be seen from the adjacent Umpqua Lighthouse State Park. The park is located off Highway 101, just south of Winchester Bay.*

---

# CAPE ARAGO LIGHT
## Charleston, Oregon – 1934

Accessible

Another seamark familiar to lumber freighters is the Cape Arago Lighthouse, located less than two miles southwest of the entrance to Coos Bay. For almost one and a half centuries, ships have sailed into the bay to take on loads of lumber and wood products. Even today the city of Coos Bay and its sister city, North Bend, are often fragrant with the aroma of freshly sawn wood. Oregon's forests still provide much of the commerce in this region, which was once known to people in the forest industry as "the softwood capital of the world."

By the time of the Civil War, Coos Bay already attracted enough seagoing traffic to require a lighthouse. In 1866 a light station was established on a small, strategically placed island just north of Cape Arago. From here it could guide ships into the bay and also serve as a marker for vessels passing up and down the Oregon coast.

The original iron tower stood for more than four decades before erosion forced the Lighthouse Board to replace it. A wooden structure built further back from the rapidly weathering cliffs, the station's second lighthouse served for only thirty years before it, too, was threatened by erosion. Completed in 1934, a third lighthouse, built of reinforced concrete, has proved more durable than its predecessors. It still

*The fourth-order lens of the Cape Arago Lighthouse shines through a thin fog. The light serves Coos Bay, famous as a lumber port.*

*Wind and water have separated the lighthouse from the mainland. The iron footbridge shown in the foreground provides access.*

stands, more than half a century after its construction, although its island perch is considerably diminished. Wind and weather are constantly cutting away the island, which is connected to the mainland by a narrow footbridge.

The octagonal concrete tower is forty-four feet tall, and together with the elevation of the island, places the fourth-order light about one hundred feet above mean sea level, making it visible from approximately sixteen miles at sea. The light is a welcome sight to mariners, for this stretch of the Oregon coast is among the rockiest and most dangerous passages for ships in American waters.

*Cape Arago and its lighthouse stand about 2 miles south of Charleston, which is located inside the entrance to Coos Bay. To reach Charleston, turn west off Highway 101 at the city of Coos Bay. The lighthouse is not open to the public.*

# COQUILLE RIVER LIGHT
## Bandon, Oregon – 1896

### Accessible

Now an attraction of Bullards Beach State Park, this little lighthouse stood empty and ignored for nearly half a century, longer, in fact, than it served as an active light station. Gutted by vandals after the Coast Guard abandoned it in 1939, it was left to deteriorate—a sorry end for a structure that saved so many ships from destruction in the treacherous shallows of the Coquille River.

In 1870 the schooner *Commodore* ran aground and broke up on the bar near the entrance of the river. Since that first wreck the list of the Coquille's victims has grown long and impressive. It includes many schooners, such as the *Randolph* (lost in 1915), the *E. L. Smith* (sunk in 1935), and the *Golden West* (foundered in 1936), as well as a large number of tugs and other vessels. Three schooners, the *Onward, Western Home,* and *Del Norte,* went down here in little more than a year, between 1904 and 1905.

*As romantically inspiring as a full moon, the restored Coquille River Lighthouse paints a bright streak over the water. This photograph was taken from Bandon, on the opposite bank of the Coquille River, with a telephoto lens.*

*Oregon boasts one of the most extensive and varied park systems in the country, as evidenced by this peaceful scene at Bullards Beach State Park near Bandon. The Coquille River Lighthouse stands in the distance.*

Most of these unfortunate vessels came to the Coquille River to take on loads of lumber harvested from Oregon's tall virgin forests. Late in the last century the lumber traffic in and out of the riverside port of Bandon became brisk, and sea captains demanded a light to help them navigate the Coquille's treacherous entrance. The bar at the mouth of the river was considered by many among the most dangerous on the West Coast.

Completed in 1895, the forty-foot lighthouse tower was made of brick protected by a layer of stucco. It was given a relatively small, fourth-order Fresnel lens. First lighted in 1896, it burned for more than four decades before it was abandoned and replaced by a series of buoys and a small jetty light.

---

*Located in Bullards Beach State Park off Highway 101 near Bandon, the lighthouse has been carefully restored and is open daily during the summer. Just across the river in Bandon are several restaurants and the Lighthouse Inn, all offering excellent views of the light.*

---

# CAPE BLANCO LIGHT
## Port Orford, Oregon – 1870

Accessible

The southernmost of Oregon's major lights is Cape Blanco. The fifty-nine-foot conical tower stands far up on the rocks of the cape, which raises the focal plane of the second-order Fresnel lens to a lofty 245 feet above mean sea level. As a result, Cape Blanco is Oregon's highest light. Its one million–candlepower flashes can be seen from twenty-two miles at sea.

The light station takes its name from the cape's precipitous white cliffs, which drop down almost vertically to the beaches below. Seen from out at sea, the cliffs are quite beautiful, especially when evening sunlight washes them with color. Mariners seldom take the time to appreciate their beauty, however, for these are among the most dangerous waters in America.

Countless vessels have piled up on the rocks along this treacherous stretch of coast. In 1883 the steamer *Victoria* foundered on the reefs off Cape Blanco. Six years later the sidewheeler *Alaskan* broke up and sank within sight of the lighthouse. Down with her went thirty of her forty-seven passengers and crew. In 1895 the 1,430-ton British steamer *Bawnmore,* carrying, of all things, a cargo of streetcars, went ashore a few miles north of the light. A fast-working lifesaving team saved the passengers and crew, but most of the streetcars were lost. No one is sure what happened to the steam schooner *South Coast,* which disappeared off Cape Blanco during a late summer storm in 1930. Carrying a heavy load of cedar logs from California, the schooner vanished, along with her entire crew of nineteen. Later the schooner's deckhouse washed ashore on the cape.

Government officials were well aware of the dangers of the cape when they commissioned construction of the lighthouse in 1868. They paid $20,000 for its powerful eight-sided, first-order Fresnel lens, which was handmade in Paris under the direction of famed lens maker Henry Lapaute. The huge lens was replaced many years ago by a second-order revolving lens seven feet high and five feet in diameter. Placed in service in December 1870, it began to warn sailors away from the cape's ship-killing rocks and reefs. Before that time mariners had to rely on their instincts and their lucky stars to get them safely past the rocks, although they sometimes got a little help from a friendly innkeeper named Louis Knapp. In harsh weather and in the winter, Knapp always kept a lantern burning in the window of his hotel near the cape. Sailors learned to look for it.

*Only recently the Coast Guard opened the gate and now allows the public to walk the grounds around the light tower. It can also be viewed from the beach at Cape Blanco State Park.*

Perhaps Knapp deserves to be known as the first lighthouse keeper in this area. But its best-known keeper was surely James Langlois, who came to Cape Blanco in 1875. With the help of two female assistants, Langlois kept the light burning for forty-two years.

*The Cape Blanco Lighthouse has a second-order Fresnel lens and attached workhouse. The tower is fifty-nine feet tall but stands on a high cliff, so the light beams toward the Pacific on a focal plane 245 feet above sea level.* **(Courtesy John. W. Weil)**

# CHAPTER THREE

# LIGHTS OF
# THE REDWOOD COAST

## Northern California

*From their lofty, cliffside perches, California lighthouses such as this one at Point Reyes offer stunning, condor's-eye views of the Pacific. The Point Reyes tower is rather squat, but it can do the work of a much taller lighthouse because it rests on a 300-foot escarpment. The equipment on the roof of the fog-signal building at the right includes a radio antenna and backup strobe lamps, which can be used if the main light fails.*

# Lights of the Redwood Coast

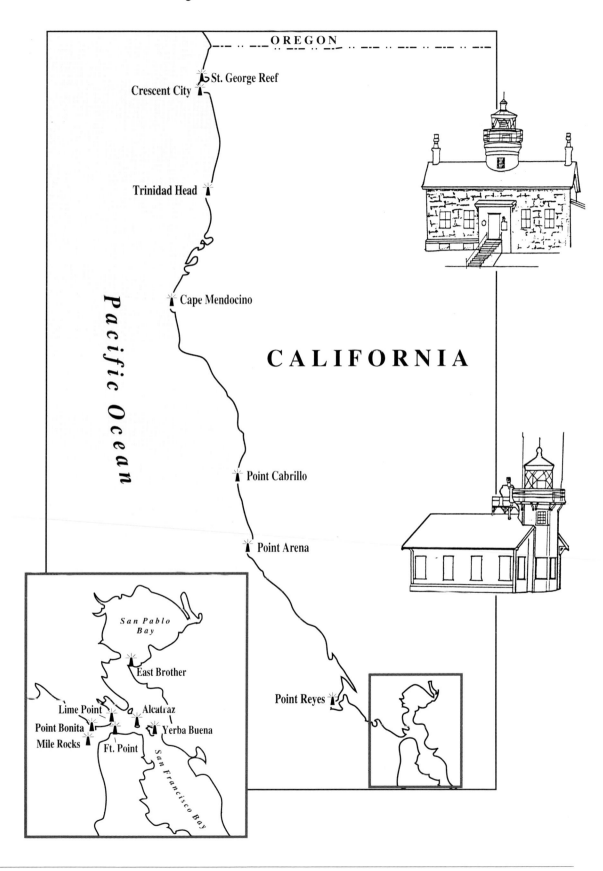

*Workers put finishing touches on the scaffolded tower of the St. George Lighthouse, shown here under construction near Crescent City, California, during the 1890s. The tower stands on a massive base made with granite blocks, each weighing more than two tons. The Olympian task of establishing a lighthouse on this exposed, wave-swept outcropping was undertaken by the same tough engineer and crew that built the Tillamook Rock Lighthouse well to the north. They completed their work at Tillamook Rock in eighteen months; but because of bad weather and funding shortages, the St. George Lighthouse took more than five years to build.*
**(Courtesy National Archives)**

## ST. GEORGE AND THE DRAGON

Some commercial fisherman still call it the Dragon. In 1792 English explorer George Vancouver gave this deadly reef the name Dragon Rocks. The name was later changed to St. George Reef. But whether medieval saint or dragon, the reef is a legend among mariners. Most consider it a monster.

St. George Reef is the peak of a submerged volcanic mountain about six miles off the extreme north coast of California. Its uppermost rocks reach just above the toss of the waves, out of sight to all but the sharpest-eyed sailor. The rocks rise abruptly from the sea, and there are no surrounding shallows to warn ships that they are approaching disaster. During rough weather, waves breaking over the rocks throw an obscuring blanket of mist over the reef, making it practically invisible.

For the passengers and crew of the Civil War–era side-wheel steamer *Brother Jonathan,* the reef was a sea monster indeed—a merciless one. Plowing through heavy weather on the way to San Francisco, the *Brother Jonathan* slammed into the reef and sank in a matter of minutes. Nearly 200 lives were lost in the calamity.

The tragic loss of the *Brother Jonathan* became something of a scandal. Why had nothing been done to mark this obvious and death-dealing maritime hazard? The *Brother Jonathan* was not the only vessel to open its hull on the reef's sharp rocks, and there had been many other deaths. A cemetery in Crescent City was filled with the graves of mariners who would have lived longer had it not been for St. George Reef. Sailors, maritime interests, and the general public demanded action.

It was not immediately clear to the Lighthouse Board what should be done, however. If a lighthouse were built, should it—or could it—be placed on the rocks themselves? Building the lighthouse directly over the reef would require an Olympian feat of engineering and construction and might be prohibitively expensive. A plan to build a mainland lighthouse on nearby St. George Point had to be abandoned because the site was shown to be too far from the reef to serve as an effective warning. Most vessels navigating this area made it a practice to run well offshore, and many of them could not see the light if its source were on the mainland.

So, after much debate and many delays, the board decided to shoulder the task of building a light tower on the exposed, wave-swept rocks of St. George Reef. To execute the daunting project, the board hired M. A. Ballantyne, who had led the conquest of Tillamook Rock only the year before. With the Tillamook Lighthouse complete—a construction project many had thought impossible—and its light burning, Ballantyne brought his crew of experienced workers south during the winter of 1882.

Aboard the 126-ton schooner *LaNinfa,* Ballantyne and his crew anchored off St. George Reef for several weeks. Weather conditions were so rough that Ballantyne's surveyors and workers managed to get onto the rocks only three times in a stretch of four weeks. But by the early spring, work was underway. Ballantyne's formidable crew of nearly fifty workmen rigged a cable from the rock's highest point—about fifty-four feet—to the schooner, which had been secured with heavy mooring tackle.

The cable served as an aerial tramway, allowing workers to slide to the rock in a breeches buoy, a life ring with canvas pants attached to the cable. Tools and equipment were transferred to the rock inside a stout cage. A small derrick and hoist on the rock helped pull the men and equipment up the tramway to the construction site, while gravity provided the power for the return trip to *LaNinfa*.

As they became used to riding over the sea, the workers started using the open cage to make trips to and from the rock. As many as six men could ride in the cage at a time, and this made it possible to evacuate the work site in a matter of minutes when dangerous storms swept in off the Pacific. While his men carved the foundation and built the inverted pyramidal base on which the light tower would stand, Ballantyne kept an eye on the seaward horizon. When swells began to build and a storm threatened, he would give the alarm and send his men gliding back over the tramway in the cage to the relative safety of *LaNinfa*.

The sea was not the only danger faced by the builders. The glycerine powder used for blasting out the foundation was highly unstable, and an accidental explosion was always a threat. What is more, the hard but brittle stone of the reef shattered easily, and the crew was often showered with sharp, shrapnel-like rock fragments when the glycerine was detonated. When blasting, the workers scurried for cover like infantrymen under attack. Despite precautions, there were frequent injuries, and even *LaNinfa* was sometimes hit by blast fragments.

The work did not progress as smoothly or steadily as it had at Tillamook. Furious storms and long stretches of generally horrible weather produced long delays. So, too, did lack of money. The original congressional appropriation had been highly unrealistic, and soon bills began to stack up faster than the stones of the light

*Like a tall ship slicing through a pounding sea, the St. George Lighthouse stands up to the Pacific. Constantly manned for more than eighty years, the lighthouse served from 1892 until 1972, when the Coast Guard abandoned the site.*
**(Courtesy National Archives)**

tower. Not until 1887 did Congress provide sufficient funds for the structure to be completed. Eventually the government spent a whopping $704,633 on the project, making this the most expensive lighthouse in the nation's history.

As work continued, a seventy-foot-high reinforced concrete pier was firmly anchored to the rock. Once the pier was finished, it became the base for a granite tower consisting of 1,339 blocks of dressed stone. The tower's heaviest blocks weighed up to two and a half tons each. The huge stones were cut and fit together with such precision that they had no more than a $^3/_{16}$-inch gap between them. Hefty metal dowels held the big stones one to another. Cement and cut stone were forced into even the smallest openings between the granite stones so that the completed tower was like a solid piece of rock.

The St. George Reef Lighthouse was at last placed in service on October 20, 1892, more than ten years after construction got underway. The station's first-order Fresnel lens shined from atop a 134-foot, square-shaped tower with a circular stairwell leading up one side to the lantern room. The keepers gained access to the stairway by passing through the boiler, coal, and laundry rooms at the base. As they climbed, they passed successive levels containing a galley, the head keeper's quarters, the assistant keepers' quarters, the watch room (later the radio room), and finally the lantern room with its enormous lens.

The station was considered too isolated and dangerous for families, so most lighthouse personnel maintained homes on the mainland. The government provided residences for families on St. George Point. The station crew consisted of five men who worked four weeks on and two weeks off. The long unrelieved stretches of work created tension between members of the station crew. On one occasion, during a month-long series of fierce storms that prevented relief personnel from reaching the rock, crew members stopped talking to one another altogether. At mealtimes they sat facing away from the table so they would not have to look at one another.

Eventually the crewmen settled their argument, but no one at Dragon Rock ever made complete peace with the sea. St. George Lighthouse developed a reputation as one of the most dangerous light stations in America. On several occasions crewmen were killed while traveling to or from the reef. In 1951 three coastguardsmen were drowned in a single incident when waves swamped the station launch.

Vancouver, the explorer who gave the reef the name Dragon Rocks, also named the nearby point after the mythical dragon slayer St. George. Perhaps he meant the names as a joke. But the dragon reef is no joke, and unlike St. George's dragon, it has never been conquered. In 1972 the Coast Guard abandoned the St. George Lighthouse and replaced it with a buoy. The reef was then left unwatched and untrammeled by humans, to carry on its ageless battle with the sea.

The big lens that once crowned the St. George Lighthouse was a Fresnel, a type first made in Paris early in the nineteenth century. Many of the old lighthouses along the West Coast still depend on their original Fresnel lenses to focus the light that mariners and more than a few delighted landlubbers see glimmering from a distance. Surprisingly, the older lenses—some of them made more than 150 years ago—are often as good or better than those manufactured today. "The Fresnels can still be used because this technology reached its zenith more than a century ago," says one coastguardsman. "There have been very few improvements since the 1850s."

# CRESCENT CITY LIGHT
## Crescent City, California – 1856

Accessible

Now a museum, the Crescent City Lighthouse once helped fuel the economy of this community situated on the far north coast of California. During the nineteenth century big trees, most of them redwoods, made the place a boomtown. The ancient trees were being cut down to build San Francisco, and the lumber was loaded onto ships in the Crescent City harbor. The lighthouse guided the lumber ships in and out and warned them of dangerous rocks near the harbor entrance.

The citizens of Crescent City were among the first in California to petition the government for a lighthouse. In 1855 Congress appropriated $15,000 to purchase a

*The silhouetted Crescent City Lighthouse can't compete with the setting sun; but after nightfall, its Fresnel lens will be the brightest star on the horizon.* (**Courtesy John W. Weil**)

tract of land and build the station. A brick tower and stone keeper's cottage were built on rocks at the end of Battery Point, about forty-five feet above the sea. As with many early California lighthouses, the tower rose through the center of the dwelling. Atop the fifty-foot tower a fourth-order Fresnel lens beamed seaward.

The station's first official keeper was Theophilus Magruder, who arrived with his wife at Battery Point on Christmas Day in 1856. A native of Washington, D.C., Magruder had led a sophisticated social life before he left the East to search for gold in Oregon. Along with his partner, John Marshall, Magruder combed the Oregon coastal mountains and panned its streams for years, never finding the precious metal he sought. Eventually the pair split up, and Marshall drifted off to the Sierra foothills, where he not only found gold but touched off the great California gold rush of 1849.

Magruder also found glitter, although not of the golden variety, by tending a gleaming new Fresnel lens at the Crescent City Lighthouse. When he could spare the time, Magruder relaxed in a chair built for him by his old partner and, no doubt, dreamed of what his life might have been like had he struck gold instead of Marshall.

As a museum maintained by the Del Norte County Historical Society, the lighthouse appears today much as it did when its lamp was first lit in 1856. It serves as a major maritime attraction and is even reputed to harbor a ghost. At least six people are said to have heard the ghost's seabooted feet slowly climbing the tower steps during severe storms.

Even if they do not meet up with the ghost, visitors will find plenty to see here. In addition to an array of early lighthouse equipment, the edifice displays artifacts from some of the less fortunate vessels that did not reach the safety of the harbor. In the main room is a bell from the steamer *Brother Jonathan,* which sank off Battery Point with a loss of 200 lives. Also on display are a number of items salvaged from the World War II tanker *Emidio,* a victim of torpedoes fired by a Japanese submarine lurking off the California coast.

---

*The Del Norte County Historical Society maintains the lighthouse as a history museum. The lighthouse stands on the west side of the harbor on Battery Point. The light shines nightly through a drum-type lens. Hours are Wednesday through Sunday, 10:00 A.M.–5:00 P.M.—when the tide is out. For more information call (707) 464–3089 or write to the society at P.O. Box 396, Crescent City, CA 95531.*

---

# TRINIDAD HEAD LIGHT
**Trinidad, California – 1871**

Accessible

Set back from a jagged cliff face 196 feet above the Pacific surf, the Trinidad Head Lighthouse has aided commercial fishermen returning to the safety of the port of Trinidad for more than a century. Trinidad Harbor nestles behind a broad headland, which absorbs most of the fury of the ocean's winter storms. Some of them are ferocious indeed.

One of the largest storm waves ever recorded struck Trinidad Head on December 31, 1914. It was observed by keeper Fred Harrington, and had the wave been only a little more powerful, neither the lighthouse nor Harrington would have survived it.

*The Trinidad Head Lighthouse has served since 1871. On the other side of these rocks is quaint Trinidad Harbor, where visitors can still buy fresh salmon from fishermen.* **(Courtesy U.S. Coast Guard)**

For more than an hour Harrington had watched the gale grow ever stronger in force, and he could see enormous waves breaking over the top of 103-foot Pilot Rock about half a mile to the south. As the keeper turned to wipe moisture from the lantern windows, he saw a mountainous sea sweeping toward the headland and the lighthouse. For a moment he stood watching in horror, but there was nothing he could do but hope for the best. Seconds later the huge wave hit the rocks, throwing a wall of green water over the lighthouse.

Windows were broken and the mechanism that rotated the light was stopped, but when the water rushed back down into the sea, the lighthouse and Harrington were still functioning. The keeper had the light flashing again in fewer than thirty minutes.

Yurok Indians were the first people known to have ventured seaward from the sheltered cove behind Trinidad Head. In the summer of 1775 the Spanish explorers Heceta and Bodega arrived to survey Humboldt Bay. By 1854 American settlements had been established, and residents petitioned Congress for a lighthouse to guide lumber boats in and out of the harbor.

In the spring of 1871 workmen carved out a shelf from the rock and started building the twenty-five-foot brick tower. The oil lamp inside the station's fourth-order Fresnel lens was first lit on December 1, 1871.

An enormous fog bell was placed on the head in 1898. The bell was so loud that its vibrations soon shook loose the weights that helped ring it, and, together with their cables, they plunged into the sea. The bell proved too strong for the replacement mechanism as well. It is easy to imagine what it did to the keeper's ears.

*Off Highway 101 about 20 miles north of Eureka, the town of Trinidad has two almost identical lighthouses, the original one, on Trinidad Head, and another, a tourist attraction, built nearer to the road for the benefit of visitors. The tourist lighthouse contains the Fresnel lens that once graced the old light tower on the head.*

# CAPE MENDOCINO LIGHT
## Capetown, California – 1909

### Observable

You can't go much farther west in the West than Cape Mendocino—it is the westernmost point in California. Towering 1,400 feet above the ocean and dropping almost vertically down to it, the cape is the highest headland in California. It is also one of the wildest, windiest, and most beautiful.

In the spring wildflowers spangle the cape's rolling, grassy hills. Narrow forests of tall trees struggle for footholds in ravines, where they find protection from the nearly constant winds. Often the wind can be heard whistling over and around Sugar Loaf, a 326-foot rock about 250 yards offshore.

The weather at Cape Mendocino is fickle, shifting quickly from fog to gale to sunshine and back to fog all in a single afternoon. The changes come with little or no warning. The contrariness of the weather here is due to a climatic peculiarity. The chilly northern current that drives the weather of northern California makes a sudden change of course off the cape, causing warm and cool air masses to mix, with highly unpredictable results.

During the 1500s Spanish galleons returning to Mexico from the Philippines used the cape to determine their position. Intending to keep well away from the cape and its perilous rock, they turned south here, making for Acapulco. Lost in fog or driven onward by the wind, more than a few turned too late and ended their days as rotting hulks on the cape's beaches.

Nowadays, sailors are warned of the cape's dangers by an automated light shining seaward from atop a polelike structure some 515 feet up the cape's west-facing slope. About seventy yards away stands the old lighthouse, which handled the same job faithfully for more than a century.

The original lighthouse is only forty-seven feet tall, but its perch 422 feet above the sea made it one of the highest marine-navigation lights in the United States.

The need for the light was dramatized on January 4, 1860, when the Pacific mail steamer *Northerner,* bound from San Francisco to the Columbia River, crashed on Two Fathoms Rock only a mile from the proposed light station. The steamer took thirty-eight passengers and crew down with her.

To build the lighthouse, crews had to carve terraces from the slope. Materials were brought ashore through the surf from a lighthouse tender and hauled up a steep, winding trail.

Once completed, the lighthouse and dwellings were far from comfortable. Fierce winter winds blew down chimneys, shattered windows, and shook the very walls. During a particularly violent storm, one assistant keeper was forced to flee his residence and take refuge in the more solidly built lighthouse tower. Another had his house almost blown apart in a storm and afterwards moved his family into the station's smelly oil house.

The wind made walking back and forth between the residences and lighthouse a

*The Cape Mendocino Lighthouse looks like an empty bird cage without its huge, first-order Fresnel lens, removed when the station was automated in 1950. Abandoned decades ago, the old tower shows the scars of time, weather, and neglect. It stands on a 380-foot promontory.* **(Courtesy U.S. Coast Guard)**

perilous adventure. Even the most surefooted keepers had to watch their step or run the risk of being blown off the cliff. A sleeping shanty was attached to the tower so keepers could avoid these hazards when gales were howling.

---

*To reach Cape Mendocino take the coast road off Highway 101 through Ferndale and Capetown. The light station is not open to the public, but enterprising travelers can get a view of it.*

---

# POINT CABRILLO LIGHT

**Mendocino, California – 1909**

Observable

When the sea is running, it slams against Point Cabrillo, hurling spray onto rocks near the top of the sixty-foot cliffs. A salty mist settles on wildflowers and the needles of cypress hedgerows that line the headland, while down below seawater rushes into a honeycomb of tunnels reaching far back under the point. Some of these tunnels cut directly beneath the Point Cabrillo Lighthouse, but for the moment at least, the ground under the station remains solid.

The point is blanketed by fog for an average of 1,000 hours a year, but often the weather is clear and the sun bright. The lighthouse was automated in the 1970s, but during the more than six decades it was manned, the good weather, rich soil, and abundant fresh water made it easy for lighthouse keepers to raise food and feed their families. Usually, they tilled large gardens and kept cows, pigs, and chickens. Easy access to schools, churches, and stores, along with its lovely pastoral setting, helped make Point Cabrillo a popular duty station.

The lighthouse itself adds to the bucolic feeling of the place. Its steeplelike tower gives it the look of a small country church. Despite its appearance, this is a hardworking yeoman of a lighthouse with more than eighty years of service to mariners.

*From a distance, the Point Cabrillo Lighthouse looks like an old country church or schoolhouse. Much of the building once housed compressors for the station's fog signal.* **(Courtesy U.S. Coast Guard)**

The lamp at the top of the forty-seven foot tower was first lit on June 10, 1909. Its third-order Fresnel lens was mounted on four tiers of brass pillars, and it rotated on chariot wheels with heavy ball bearings.

It was the lumber industry that petitioned the government to build the Point Cabrillo Lighthouse, so it is perhaps not surprising that all of the station's buildings were made of wood. With the tower rising from its roof, the main structure suggests the Cape Cod style of California's earliest lighthouses. Painted white with gray trim, it was given a red roof and black lantern.

The largest portion of the building once housed the big gas engines and air compressors that powered the station's two fog signals. Facing seaward, the horns protruded through the roof of the building. They resembled the trumpet-shaped exhausts of below-decks ventilators on ships. During the 1980s the foghorns were removed, and a sound buoy took over their task of warning sailors away from the point's dangerous rocks. Many ships have been lost along this treacherous stretch of coast, more than a few of them schooners and freighters carrying lumber harvested from the area's once dense forests. These slow-moving vessels were particularly vulnerable to storms that howled out of the north and east without warning. Unwary crews often found themselves driven onto the rocks.

*In this early view of the Point Cabrillo Lighthouse, notice the twin fog-signal horns protruding from the roof.* **(Courtesy U.S. Coast Guard)**

In February 1960 one such storm almost carried away the lighthouse itself. It was a gale of such violence that two-ton boulders were torn away from the cliff face and thrown shoreward. Enormous waves surged up the sides of the cliff and swept over the grass, slamming into the heavy doors at the seaward end of the building. Soon the doors caved in, and a huge generator was ripped from its floor bolts and shoved against the far wall. When the sea retreated the following day, it left a foot of gravel and sand on the floor.

*Located off California Route 1 near Mendocino, the Point Cabrillo Light Station is closed to the public. The glorious old frame lighthouse can be viewed from the highway, however.*

# POINT ARENA LIGHT
**Point Arena, California – 1870**

Accessible

Motorists driving along California Route 1 north of San Francisco are struck by the gentle appearance of the landscape. They see green fields running right down to the edge of the blue Pacific and small herds of contented cattle and sheep grazing in rich pastures covered by thick carpets of grass. The rugged mountains just to the east form a wall that seems to protect this pastoral Shangri-la from the rest of the world and its worries. Usually, the most threatening thing one encounters here is an occasional California highway patrol car.

Mariners see this shoreline differently, however. For them it is fraught with dangers—rocks and reefs waiting to destroy any ship that strays off course.

Like most of this coastline, Point Arena turns a hospitable face to those who

*The steep, rocky cliffs below the Point Arena Lighthouse show how California's fault lines have scarred and twisted the land. Not surprisingly, the ocean bottom off this coast is littered with sharp, ship-killing rocks and reefs.*

came by land but bares its teeth to sailors. Some two and a half miles offshore, predatory Point Arena Rock rises from the sea, waiting to tear open the stoutest hulls. For the unwary, Point Arena Lighthouse flashes out its two million–candle-power warning: "Don't come too close."

Now fully automated, the light was first lit on May 1, 1870. The original station had two twelve-inch-diameter steam whistles protruding from its fog-signal building. The steam for the whistles was generated by wood-burning boilers that consumed up to 100 tons of firewood during especially foggy years.

The station's outbuildings included a barn, laundry shed, and hen house, all spotlessly whitewashed, as were the fog-signal building and the lighthouse. Like Point Arena itself, the station had an idyllic outward appearance, but when seen from another angle, it was somewhat less hospitable. Keepers had to share the two-and-a-half-story residence with three assistants, together with all their wives and children. The arrangement afforded little privacy and even less peace and quiet, as noted in an 1880 log entry: "Threatening weather and fighting children."

Keepers complained about the cramped living conditions but were ignored. It took an earthquake to bring improvements. On April 18, 1906, the trembling earth leveled much of San Francisco and devastated the Point Arena Lighthouse. While the station was being rebuilt, the keepers and their families had to live in tents. But much to their relief, the repair effort included construction of four new, freestanding residences.

The new light tower saw improvements as well. It was raised to a height of 115 feet—the original tower had been 100 feet tall. Builders employed reinforced concrete, a revolutionary technique in lighthouse construction, but one that would become standard.

Because of the threat of earthquakes, the Point Arena tower was secured by massive concrete buttresses at its base. This gave the tower the appearance of an obelisk standing on a pedestal but also made it very strong. It has survived numerous earth tremors and even a brush with a navy dirigible.

---

*To reach Point Arena Lighthouse take Lighthouse Road north from the town of Point Arena. The local Lighthouse Keepers Association offers tours of the lighthouse and fog-signal buildings. The lighthouse is open 10:00 A.M.–3:30 P.M. from May 30 to Labor Day and 11:00 A.M.–2:30 P.M. during the rest of the year. For more information call (707) 882–2777 or write P.O. Box 11, Point Arena, CA 95468.*

---

# POINT REYES LIGHT

**Point Reyes National Seashore, California – 1870**

Accessible

Lighthouse keepers never considered Point Reyes among the most desirable duty stations, and it is not hard to see why. The winds howl constantly, there are frequent driving rains, and the point is socked in by an incredible 2,700 hours of fog a year. Added to the discomforts of wind and weather were the 638 steps that had to be climbed to reach the tower and foghorn house from the keeper's dwelling.

Perhaps after a particularly taxing climb in the teeth of yet another ferocious gale, keeper E. G. Chamberlain wrote the following poetic lines in 1885: "Solitude, where are the charms that sages have seen in thy face? Better dwell in the midst of alarms then reign in this horrible place."

With the coming of electricity, modern communications systems, and improved transportation, the lot of Point Reyes keepers improved. But the horrible weather and winds, sometimes clocked in excess of 100 miles per hour, at the very least kept them acquainted with their former miseries. The station was finally automated in 1975, much to the relief, no doubt, of some wind-battered keeper. Today the property is maintained by the National Park Service as a historic site.

*Frequently torn by high winds, rugged Point Reyes is one of the foggiest places in America. The lighthouse has been warning ships since 1870.*

Although it reaches an elevation of more than 600 feet at one location, most of Point Reyes is relatively low. A narrow finger of land, it curves seaward for ten miles. From the sea its highest point often appears to be an island rising abruptly from the water. This illusion has lured more than one vessel to destruction.

In 1595 the Spanish ship *San Agustin,* bound from the Philippines to Acapulco, Mexico, with 130 tons of cargo and a crew of seventy, sought shelter here from a storm. Instead of safe harbor the ship found dangerous shallows and ran aground in Drake's Bay. The vessel's Portuguese master, Captain Sebastian Rodriguez Cermeno, had to fight a war with the local Indians to salvage what he could from the ruined ship. In spite of his best efforts, most of the cargo and food supplies were lost, along with twelve of his men.

Despite the *San Agustin* wreck and many other disasters that followed, Point Reyes remained unmarked for more than 275 years. Congress authorized construction of a lighthouse on Point Reyes in 1852, but government officials spent seventeen years wrangling with local owners over the price of land. Not until 1869 was the Lighthouse Board able to purchase a site—120 acres for $6,000. The price included rights to firewood and water as well as access to a nearby granite quarry.

By the late fall of 1870, a forty-foot-high, sixteen-sided tower encased in iron plate stood on the point, some 294 feet above the sea. The two-ton, first-order Fresnel lens was put in place, and on the night of December 1 the lamp was lit.

*(Top) The Point Reyes fog signals and compressors are well maintained. (Below) This brass plaque adorns the base of the station's elegant, Parisian Fresnel lens.*

*The Point Reyes Lighthouse is located at Point Reyes National Seashore, off California Route 1 northwest of San Francisco. This wild seashore is home to fox, elk, and even mountain lions. There is also an Indian village, and the point is a good spot to watch for migrating gray whales. The squat lighthouse clings to a narrow rocky point. Access to more than 300 steps leading down to the lighthouse is sometimes prohibited because of the wind. Views are frequently obscured by fog. Point Reyes is, in fact, one of the foggiest places in the United States. Visitors should begin at the Bear Valley visitors' center, near the seashore entrance. For information and hours call (415) 669–1534.*

# LIGHTHOUSES OF SAN FRANCISCO BAY

**Alcatraz Island – 1909**

**Fort Point – 1855**

**East Brother – 1874**

**Point Bonita – 1877**

Accessible

**Yerba Buena – 1874**

**Lime Point – 1900**

**Mile Rocks – 1906**

Inaccessible

For lighthouse lovers San Francisco is a feast. The San Francisco Bay area boasts the West Coast's oldest lighthouse, on Alcatraz Island, and several other major navigational lights. Among the gems in this sparkling necklace of beacons are the Point Bonita, Mile Rocks, and Lime Point lighthouses near the Golden Gate and the Yerba Buena, East Brother, and Alcatraz lighthouses, all on islands in the bay itself. The old skeleton-style lighthouse at Fort Point still stands but is no longer active.

A robust frontier port in the mid-1800s, San Francisco was the funnel through which countless thousands of doggedly optimistic Americans passed on their way to the gold fields in the Sierra foothills. Only a tiny percentage of California's forty-niners turned their golden dreams into real, bankable riches. The West, however,

*Suggesting a ruined medieval fortress, the Alcatraz penitentiary is now abandoned, but the island's lighthouse remains active.*
**(Courtesy U.S. Coast Guard)**

*(Above) Lovely Point Bonita Lighthouse is reached by a small but handsome suspension bridge. (Below left) Fort Point Lighthouse stands atop a pre–Civil War fortress.* **(Fort Point photo courtesy John W. Weil)**

was a big place with such an abundance of land and resources that anybody with a little hard work and horse sense could make himself at least *feel* rich.

Very early on people began to see the San Francisco Bay as the door to the West. Through the Golden Gate, with its Gibraltarlike ramparts, would flow the settlers and materials needed to populate and build up a new and prosperous region. Recognizing this, Congress approved and appropriated funds to build one lighthouse after another to guide ships into San Francisco's harbor or up the Sacramento River.

The first to be built were the Alcatraz Island and Fort Point lighthouses. Begun in 1852, they were completed the following year, but the tower at Fort Point was torn down to make way for a military garrison before it was ever used. The Alcatraz station was not placed in operation until June 1854, shortly after its third-order Fresnel lens was delivered from France. Nonetheless, this still made Alcatraz the first active lighthouse in the West.

The original Cape Cod–style dwelling and tower on

*Not so graceful as the city of San Francisco, shown here peeking through a mist, the Lime Point Lighthouse nonetheless performs its task—saving ships and lives.*

Alcatraz served well for more than sixty years before suffering serious damage in the 1906 San Francisco earthquake. Soon thereafter the island was put to another, darker use as a maximum-security prison where some of the nation's most notorious criminals were incarcerated. The prison's high walls partially blocked the beacon of the old, badly shaken lighthouse, so it was torn down and replaced by a taller structure.

An eighty-four-foot octagonal tower of reinforced concrete was erected outside the prison walls. The new lighthouse was completed and relit in 1909. The elevation of the island placed the focal plane of the light 214 feet above sea level. The station's lovely, two-story, bay-style dwelling was burned during an extraordinary invasion by Indian protesters in 1970. Automated since 1963, the light still shines every night and, for many, remains an important symbol for the city.

A new lighthouse was eventually built at Fort Point outside the walls of Fort Winfield Scott. Fitted with a small fifth-order lens, it was lighted in 1855. Erosion soon undercut the structure, forcing construction of yet another light tower in 1864. The third Fort Point Lighthouse was a twenty-seven-foot iron skeleton supporting a watch room and lantern room atop the walls of the fort. The light guided ships into San Francisco Bay until 1934, when the Golden Gate Bridge made it obsolete. Towering 740 feet above the sea, the bridge is itself a kind of lighthouse. Mariners can see its lights or recognize the distinct inverted arches of its supporting cables from dozens of miles at sea.

*The upper building of the Yerba Buena Island Lighthouse is the former keeper's dwelling, used today as a residence by a high-ranking Coast Guard officer. The structure below the tower once housed a powerful steam fog whistle.* (**Courtesy U.S. Coast Guard**)

In 1873–74 the Lighthouse Board established light stations in the bay at East Brother Island to the north of Alcatraz and on Yerba Buena Island to the south. Both lights still shine and are familiar to sailors whose ships regularly ply the waters of the bay. Yerba Buena was once known for the large herds of goats that ran wild over the island.

Lights were later added at Lime Point in 1900 and Mile Rocks in 1906. Both located near the Golden Gate, they helped guide ships past dangerous obstacles at the entrance to San Francisco Bay. Even today both remain indispensable to shipping.

Just outside the bay stands another veteran of frontier times, the Point Bonita Lighthouse. Lighted in the spring of 1855, it joined the neighboring Alcatraz Island Light as one of the first navigational beacons on the West Coast. The original structure was replaced by the present lighthouse in 1877. Today it stands within the Golden Gate National Recreation Area and is frequently visited by hikers.

*Listed on the National Register of Historic Places, the East Brother Lighthouse serves today as both a navigational light and a bed and breakfast inn. The B & B offers accommodations for up to four couples. The lights in the distance on the far left mark the San Rafael Bridge.*

*The **Alcatraz Island** Lighthouse is open to the public daily and can be reached by boat from Fisherman's Wharf. The lighthouse and the island's notorious prison are now part of the Golden Gate National Recreational Area. The **East Brother** Lighthouse is open to the public and operates as a bed-and-breakfast inn. The **Fort Point** Lighthouse is now part of a National Historic Site encompassing old Fort Winfield Scott and is open daily. In a detached portion of this area, off Highway 101 just north of the city, stands the **Point Bonita** Lighthouse. To reach the point from San Francisco, cross the Golden Gate Bridge and take the first (Alexander Avenue) exit. Then take Conzelman Road and follow signs to the lighthouse. The winding road to Point Bonita provides spectacular views of San Francisco. Reaching the lighthouse requires a hike of 1½ miles each way. The **Mile Rocks** and **Lime Point** lighthouses are inaccessible to the public, as is the **Yerba Buena** Lighthouse, where the old keeper's quarters now serve as home for a high-ranking Coast Guard official.*

# CHAPTER FOUR

# LIGHTS OF
# THE GOLDEN SHORES

## Southern California

*Ocean blue, red tile roof, and green palm fronds complement the white walls of the Point Vicente Lighthouse near Los Angeles.*

# Lights of the Golden Shores

Point Montara
Pigeon Point
Santa Cruz
South Farallon
Point Pinos
Point Sur

CALIFORNIA

Piedras Blancas

*Pacific Ocean*

Point Arguello
Santa Barbara
Point Conception

Anacapa Island

Point Vincente
Point Fermin
Los Angeles Harbor

Old Point Loma
Point Loma

MEXICO

*In this rather fanciful view of the South Farallon Light station, notice the armed men in the lower right-hand corner. The drawing was made during the 1850s at a time when San Francisco poachers warred over the rich harvest of eggs they stole from island sea birds.* **(Courtesy National Archives)**

The urgent need for lighthouses along the nation's newly acquired and dangerous West Coast first became apparent during the gold rush. Ships crammed with fervently hopeful prospectors and other would-be millionaires arrived in California daily during and after the height of the big rush in 1849. Most of these ships deposited their human cargo at San Francisco, but to get there they first had to pass by the rocky Farallon Islands, which rose out of the open Pacific about twenty-three miles from California's famed Golden Gate. The islands served as a signpost pointing the way to San Francisco Bay, but they were also a deadly hazard. Many fine vessels and brave seamen met their end on the sharp Farallon rocks. So when Congress selected locations for the West's first lighthouses during the early 1850s, the Farallons stood near the top of the list.

Ironically, a group of rowdy gold rush freebooters, nearly all of whom had reached California by sea, did their best to scuttle plans for a lighthouse in the Farallons. It seemed these particular forty-niners were more interested in eggs than in gold, and they saw the U.S. government and its Lighthouse Service as claim jumpers.

## THE GREAT FARALLON EGG WAR

In San Francisco chicken eggs were as scarce as hens' teeth and were selling for upwards of a dollar each. These extraordinary prices touched off a new sort of rush as bands of armed men set sail for the Farallons, where seabirds nested in vast rookeries. There they robbed the nests of hapless murres and gulls and took the eggs back to the city, where they cashed them in for considerable sums. Many of these "egg miners" were unsuccessful prospectors. Having found no gold in their pans, they resolved to provide some gold—at a respectable profit—for the frying pans of their fellow gold diggers.

Then came the U.S. Lighthouse Service with plans for a light station on Southeast Farallon, the largest of the islands. The nest robbers were convinced that a flashing navigational light and fog signal here would drive away the seabirds and ruin their burgeoning egg business. The jagged rocks of the seven-mile-long island chain threatened destruction and death to increasing numbers of ships, crews, and passengers headed for the Golden Gate, but this was of little concern to the egg gatherers. They were businessmen, and this was the West—the land of opportunity.

The forty-niner egg men were not the first to exploit the island wildlife. The name *Farallons* is derived from the description given the islands in the logbooks of early Spanish explorers, who called them *los Farallons,* meaning the "small, pointed islands." No doubt the Spanish, too, gathered eggs from the abundant nests of seabirds. In 1579 the buccaneer and globe-circling explorer Sir Francis Drake reputedly stopped here so his crew could gather eggs and harpoon seals to restock his ship's empty larder. Beginning in 1810 Russian sealing expeditions from Alaska set

*This aerial view of the South Farallon Light depicts the station as it looked in 1925.* **(Courtesy National Archives)**

up camp in the Farallons. By the end of their third hunting season in the islands, they had taken 200,000 seal pelts. In 1819 and 1820 Americans hunted sea lions here and salted the meat to feed U.S. soldiers in the Oregon Territory. But none of this activity compared with the intense rapaciousness of the gold rush egg gatherers. In a single boatload they carried off 12,000 eggs to San Francisco.

So lucrative was the egg business that various groups of poachers fell into fierce competition. Brawls and gunfights broke out when rival gangs encountered one another amid the rocks, nests, and bird droppings of the Farallons. Their battles grew so frequent and so intense that collectively they became known as the Farallon Island Egg War. The combatants even wore uniforms—baggy shirts fitted with huge pockets for gathering eggs.

In 1852 the bark *Oriole* arrived off Southeast Farallon, the largest of the islets, with a construction crew and a load of materials for building lighthouses. The vessel and the workers were turned back by an angry mob of gun-toting egg-shirted poachers.

At this the Lighthouse Service decided to get tough and dispatched a steamer, loaded not just with construction materials but with a detachment of well-armed troops. When the egg pickers saw this impressive show of force, they backed down, and construction of the light station commenced. But hostile pickers, whose activities were eventually consolidated under the umbrella of the Farallon Egg Company, continued to make a nuisance of themselves for at least twenty-five years.

Even as the pickers continued to rob nests, workmen began the exhausting task of quarrying rock from the island to form the shell of a forty-one-foot tower. Stone and bricks were lugged to the construction site near the 317-foot summit of a hill on Southeast Farallon. A dwelling for the keeper was built on a level area nearer the sea. By 1853 everything was in place but the light.

One year later a French freighter arrived in San Francisco with a most welcome cargo—a large shipment of wine and a sparkling new first-order Fresnel lens for the Farallon Lighthouse. As it turned out, however, the enormous, eight-foot diameter lens proved much too big for the light tower and its lantern room. The construction contractors, partners Kelly and Gibbons from Baltimore, were forced to tear down the tower and rebuild it from the ground up. As a consequence of the delay, the light was not in place and ready to be lit until January 1, 1856, more than three years after the project was launched.

Two years later a much-needed fog signal was added. The signal was of a revolutionary design: It was powered by air forced through a blowhole by natural wave action. Like many clever innovations, this one had an unexpected and critical flaw. On the California coast fog is usually accompanied by flat calms. As a result, when the fog signal was most needed, it barely functioned if at all. Despite its questionable usefulness, the blowhole foghorn remained in operation until storm waves smashed the contraption in 1871 and it was replaced by a more conventional steam-powered fog signal.


## THE SECOND EGG WAR

The fears of the egg pickers proved unjustified. The murres and gulls ignored the blat of the foghorn, the flashing light, and even the quarrelsome poachers who continually robbed their nests. Vast flocks continued to nest on the remote Farallons.

Some of the light station's early keepers joined in the poaching to earn a little extra "egg" money. They also hunted seals, whose powdered whiskers were sold in San Francisco's Chinatown as an aphrodisiac.

In 1881 the egg wars, quieted by the formation of the Farallon Egg Company, flared up once again. A rival group of egg pickers deeply resented the company's domination of the Farallon nests and resolved to break its monopoly. The dispute came to a head when several boatloads of armed men landed on the islands and a pitched battle ensued. The gunfire brought a din of protests from thousands of squawking seabirds. It also brought to the islands a U.S. marshall and a platoon of soldiers, who promptly evicted the trigger-happy egg pickers and burned their huts.

Nonetheless, egg picking on the Farallons continued well into the 1890s. The Lighthouse Service reached the end of its patience when an assistant keeper fell and broke both of his legs while helping the pickers gather eggs. Soon afterward the service decreed that no one be allowed to land on the islands without prior written approval from the District Superintendent of Lighthouses in San Francisco. Still the poachers came, despite occasional confrontations with keepers and police. Finally, it

*Another of the West's great island lights is the **Anacapa Island Lighthouse** off Ventura. The present cylindrical masonry tower has stood since 1932, when it replaced an earlier iron structure built in 1912. Now fully automated, the lighthouse is part of the Channel Islands National Park.* **(Courtesy U.S. Coast Guard)**

*The Anacapa Island Lighthouse is less accessible than most, since it is located several miles off the California mainland in what is now the Channel Islands National Park. The park, much of which is included in a protected "ecological reserve," can be reached only by boat. For information about transportation to the islands, call Island Packers at (805) 966–7107 in Ventura. Most of the tour boats that visit the islands operate out of Ventura Harbor.*

was not lawmen but the prodigious egg-laying capacity of California chickens that put an end to the poaching. People started eating chicken eggs by the dozen, and the market for the seabird variety dwindled to nothing.

The Farallons became a bird sanctuary in 1909. Today the islands are visited mostly by naturalists and bird fanciers who probably don't eat gulls' eggs for breakfast.

## THE LONELINESS OF ISLAND KEEPERS

The disappearance of the egg pickers left only the birds, seals, lighthouse keepers, and their families on the islands. The loneliness of this remote light station, more than twenty miles from land, soon became legendary. For many years supply boats called on the island only four times annually.

Sometimes the families of keepers suffered because of their isolation. The government had trouble hiring teachers for the keepers' children. The stir-crazy teachers usually resigned and left the islands within months of accepting the job. Tragically, at least three sick children died on Southeast Farallon because their parents could not get them to the mainland in time to receive proper medical attention.

Gradually, life at the Farallon Lighthouse improved. During World War I the navy placed a communication station on the Farallons, and navy tugs made frequent visits. Radios brought music and dance parties, and the keepers even built a tennis court. When the last keeper was removed at the time the station was automated in 1972, he was probably very sorry to go. After all, isolation can be splendid.

The Farallon Islands lie very near the imaginary line that, in the minds of most, divides northern and southern California. Because of the role they played in the great California gold rush, these islands serve as an appropriate gateway to the "Golden Shores."

# POINT MONTARA LIGHT
### Pacifica, California – 1900

Accessible

In 1868 the steamer *Colorado* ran aground on a ledge within sight of Point Montara. Four years later the freighter *Acuelo* wrecked just below the point, spilling into the sea a cargo of coal and iron worth at least $150,000. The latter disaster led to the placement of a fog signal on Point Montara in 1872. Nearly three decades would pass before the Point Montara fog-signal station became a full-fledged lighthouse.

Perched atop a thirty-foot conical tower (which replaced an earlier structure in 1928), the Point Montara Light shines from a point seventy feet above the sea. The light can be seen from about fourteen miles away. Ironically, the original fog-signal building has been removed.

*For nearly three decades Point Montara had only a fog signal to warn sailors of its jagged rocks, but in 1900 a lighthouse was added. The light still burns today, but most of the station's buildings are now used as a youth hostel.*

*Most of the buildings at the station, including the Victorian keeper's quarters, are now used as a youth hostel. Visitors hours on the grounds are limited: 7:30–9:30 A.M. and 4:30–9:30 P.M. For more information call (415) 728–7177.*

# PIGEON POINT LIGHT
## Pescadero, California – 1872

### Accessible

Fifty miles south of San Francisco, the light at Pigeon Point shines out toward the Pacific from an elevation of nearly 160 feet. Slightly more than forty feet of that height is provided by the point, the rest by the 115-foot brick tower.

The tower, one of the tallest on the Pacific Coast, was built in 1872 with brick shipped around Cape Horn from the East. The land, lighthouse, and huge first-order Fresnel lens cost the government approximately $20,000.

Pigeon Point got its name when the Yankee clipper *Carrier Pigeon* wrecked on its rocks in 1853. The 175-foot clipper had been launched in Bath, Maine, the previous year. She was 129 days out of Boston and bound for San Francisco when she ran into a thick fog off the California coast. The ship's captain, Azariah Doane, mistook the point for the Farallon Islands well to the north. The error cost Doane his ship as she ran aground on the point's sharp rocks. Before Doane and his sailors could free her, the *Carrier Pigeon* was pounded to pieces by a gale. What was left of the cargo was sold at the scene of the wreck for a fraction of its original value.

---

*Now open to the public as a hostelry, the Pigeon Point Light Station is located south of Pescadero and just north of the Ano Nuevo Reserve. The grounds are open all year. A docent leads tours on Sundays from 11:00 A.M. to 3:00 P.M. For information call (415) 879–0633.*

---

*Because, in 1853, a freighter called the* Carrier Pigeon *crashed on the rocks near here, the place has since been known as Pigeon Point. The imposing, 115-foot tower of the Pigeon Point Lighthouse has stood since 1872.*

# SANTA CRUZ LIGHT
## Santa Cruz, California – 1869

Accessible

A lighthouse stood on this site as early as 1869. This impressive brick edifice at the entrance to Santa Cruz Harbor serves both as a harbor marker and a memorial to earlier lighthouses and their keepers.

*The little brick lighthouse at the popular seaside-resort town of Santa Cruz now houses, of all things, a surfing museum.*

*The Santa Cruz Lighthouse, rebuilt in 1967, can be reached by driving northwest along West Cliff Drive to Lighthouse Point. The brick structure is now the prime attraction of the Santa Cruz Lighthouse Park and houses a surfing museum. Admission is free. The beaches in this area are excellent for strolling and offer a fine view of the lighthouse. Hours are 12:00–4:00 p.m. weekdays except Tuesday, when museum is closed, and 12:00–5:00 p.m. on weekends.*

# POINT PINOS LIGHT
## Pacific Grove, California – 1855

Accessible

Now surrounded by a golf course, the West Coast's oldest standing lighthouse is leased by the Coast Guard to a historical society, which uses it as a maritime museum. The forty-three-foot tower rises from the center of the keeper's dwelling, originally granite faced but overlaid with reinforced concrete following a severe shaking by the 1906 San Francisco Earthquake. Dormers and a rear roof have been added to the dwelling, but the tower still houses the original light.

Nestled on a southerly point on the Monterey Peninsula at the entrance to Monterey Bay, the Point Pinos Lighthouse has attracted many visitors since it was first lighted on February 1, 1855. Among the best-known tourists to enjoy a visit here was Robert Louis Stevenson, author of such classic novels as *Treasure Island* and *Dr. Jekyll and Mr. Hyde.* A popular travel writer as well as a novelist, Stevenson

*The Point Pinos dwelling and tower reflect the rather incongruous Cape Cod–style architecture of California's first lighthouses.*

came here in 1871. The keeper, Captain Allen Luce, guided Stevenson around the lighthouse property and even took time out to show the writer his ship models. Stevenson was so charmed by his visit that he included a description of the lighthouse in his travel book *The Old Pacific Coast.*

The first keeper to serve at Point Pinos was an adventurer. An Englishman, Charles Layton had fought honorably for both the British and American armies before he joined in the California gold rush of 1849. But like so many other would-be gold millionaires, Layton found little of value in the gold fields. In 1852 he gave up the search and settled in Monterey with his wife Charlotte. Within a few years he had won appointment as keeper of the Point Pinos Lighthouse at an annual salary of $1,000 a year—a comfortable sum at the time.

Layton did not live to enjoy his good fortune, however. A few months after he started, he joined a posse chasing the *bandito* Anastasio García. Layton died from a wound he received in a shootout with García and his men. As often happened when lighthouse keepers died or became incapacitated, his wife took over his duties. Mrs. Layton faithfully maintained the light and soon was appointed keeper herself.

---

*Located on Lighthouse Avenue between Sunset Drive and Asilomar Avenue in Pacific Grove, the Point Pinos Lighthouse is open to the public only on Saturday and Sunday, 1:00–4:00 P.M. For more information call the Pacific Grove Museum at (408) 372–4212 or (408) 648–3160. To reach the lighthouse take California 68 West off Highway 1, then turn left at Asilomar. Sea otters often play in the surf in this area. Nearby Monterey offers one of the world's finest public aquariums.*

---

# POINT SUR LIGHT
### Big Sur, California – 1889

Accessible

For those who love natural beauty, the stretch of California Route 1 from San Simeon to Monterey ranks among the wonders of the world. Here the continent has thrown up a wall separating its desert valleys from the Pacific. Often hundreds of feet above the pounding surf, the narrow highway clings precariously to the escarpment of the Santa Lucia Mountains. Turnouts and roadside parks offer views usually available only to eagles or condors.

Located about thirty miles south of Monterey, the tiny town of Big Sur is a magnet for backpackers and nature-loving suburbanites. Timeless coastal redwoods hide here, protected from power saws by Pfeiffer State Park. Not nearly so old as the big trees, but nonetheless venerable, is the Point Sur Lighthouse, just to the north of the town. Established in 1889, the light warns sailors not to come too close to this dangerous coastline where mountains wrestle with the ocean.

The lighthouse stands at the summit of a steep-sided sandstone island connected to the mainland by a sandy causeway. Together with the 200-foot elevation of the hill, the fifty-foot stone tower places the light more than 250 feet above sea level.

Building the lighthouse atop the rugged hill proved challenging and expensive. Congress appropriated $50,000 for the project, but contractors spent that much and more. Before construction could move forward, a railroad track had to be laid to move materials to the site.

Once the lighthouse was completed and placed in operation, the tracks were removed, and the station could only be reached by climbing a staircase of 395 steps. Keepers developed strong leg muscles, especially since the station dwelling was located a considerable distance from the light tower. Later a tramway was installed, and eventually a winding roadway was cut through to the summit to make access easier.

*Point Sur Lighthouse winks at the Pacific.*

*The lighthouse is located off California Route 1 in Pfeiffer Big Sur State Park on a sharply elevated point near the town of Big Sur. Excellent views of the light can be had when traveling south along Highway 1 from Monterey and Carmel. For those who want a closer look, tours are available on Sundays. With its scenery, redwoods, hiking, and camping, nearby Big Sur is legendary. For information call the Big Sur Chamber of Commerce at (408) 667–2100.*

# PIEDRAS BLANCAS LIGHT
## San Simeon, California – 1875

### Inaccessible

The old Piedras Blancas Lighthouse appears decapitated, as if the wing of a low-flying airplane had chopped off its lantern. Indeed, the tower was once crowned by a handsome lantern, but it was lopped off the building in 1949 when the Coast Guard removed the station's first-order Fresnel lens and replaced it with a beacon much like those used at airports.

Completed in 1875, the cone-shaped brick tower once stood ninety feet tall on a grassy knoll that lifted its light 142 feet above sea level. Today, it is about twenty feet shorter. The modern-looking beacon seems out of place on the trunk of the old tower, but it boasts an extraordinary 1.4 million candlepower, making it visible from about eighteen miles at sea.

The Piedras Blancas beacon marks the halfway point between major coastal lights at Point Conception to the south and Pigeon Point to the north. The original lens, with its multiple bull's-eyes, now stands—rather forlornly—in a small park beside California Route 1 in Cambria. Sunlight has begun to discolor the glass.

The station's fog signal, in operation since 1906, is one of the most powerful in the West. Its warning blasts are notoriously earsplitting.

*The Piedras Blancas Lighthouse was impressive before it was turned into an ugly duckling by automation. The lantern room was removed in 1949, an act which, in effect, decapitated the structure.*

*The Piedras Blancas Light Station is located off California Route 1 north of San Simeon. The views of the Pacific along this stretch of highway are truly extraordinary. Access to the lighthouse, however, is currently restricted.*

# POINT CONCEPTION LIGHT

## Point Conception, California – 1856 and 1882

### Inaccessible

California has an elbow known as Point Conception. Here, ocean currents collide to produce some of America's worst coastal weather. Some mariners consider it to be a North American version of South America's infamous Cape Horn, where gales howl in the faces of sailors trying desperately to round it.

Spanish ships sailing westward out of the Pacific were always glad to see the point after months at sea, but it did not always offer them an amiable welcome. The ocean floor off Point Conception is littered with the remains of vessels from American, Spanish, and many other nation's ports. It is not known how many ships have gone down in the waters off the point. Many of them simply disappeared, leaving no trace and no one to mourn their crews except their wives, families, and friends, who watched for them in vain.

Aware of the point's nightmarish reputation, government officials selected it as a site for one of the West's first lighthouses. Construction of the tower and keeper's dwelling began in 1854, but the station was not in operation until 1856.

The contractors hired to build the lighthouse had great difficulty getting materials to the isolated point. Once the structure was complete, inspectors found the workmanship shoddy—the mortar between the bricks was already crumbling. What was worse, the tower was obviously too small to accommodate the first-order Fresnel lens and lighting apparatus purchased for the lantern. The contractors were

*One of the West's earliest lighthouses stood on this high promontory. It was replaced by a second tower, the current Point Conception Light Station, in 1882.* **(Courtesy U.S. Coast Guard)**

forced to tear down the building and start over again, this time, no doubt, using better-quality mortar.

Meanwhile, there were delays in shipping the station's huge lens from Europe. For months the new lighthouse stood empty. When keeper George Parkinson arrived, he discovered that not only was his lighthouse without a lens, but a band of Indians had set up camp in the building. Employing a combination of threats, salty language, and other forms of persuasion, Parkinson was eventually able to evict the squatters.

In September 1855 the lamp and lens arrived by schooner, but several key parts were missing. They were not located for several months, and the keeper had to wait until February before he could finally display his light.

Parkinson and later keepers found the isolated Point Conception Lighthouse a "hardship" duty station. The nearest markets and stores were in Santa Barbara, more than sixty miles away, causing Parkinson to complain that the cost of shipping in supplies amounted to more than his government salary.

In 1875 Parkinson noticed a series of large cracks opening in the tower walls. Perhaps, after all, the construction work had not been solid. After an inspection team visited the site, the Lighthouse Board decided to abandon the structure and build another lighthouse about 100 feet lower in elevation than the first. By locating the light lower on the point, they hoped to avoid the low-hanging clouds that had frequently obscured its predecessor.

*The Point Conception Lighthouse is inaccessible to the public.*

Obviously, the second Point Conception Lighthouse was better built than the first. Completed in 1882, the fifty-two-foot tower still stands and still guides mariners with its flashing light.

*In 1934 the **Point Arguello Lighthouse,** shown here as it looked in 1902, was replaced by a forty-eight-foot skeleton tower displaying a one-million-candlepower light. Like its neighbor on Point Conception, the Point Arguello Lighthouse is inaccessible to the public.* (**Courtesy National Archives**)

# SANTA BARBARA LIGHT
## Santa Barbara, California – 1926

Accessible

One of the West Coast's earliest light stations, the Santa Barbara Lighthouse began operation in 1856. A relatively modest structure with a light tower rising through the center of the keeper's dwelling, it was much less costly than some of its cousins elsewhere along the Pacific Coast. Builder George Nagle of San Francisco received only $8,000 for completing the project—compared to the more than $38,000 bill for the Tatoosh Island (Cape Flattery) light built at about the same time.

Despite its bargain-basement price tag, the lighthouse served faithfully for nearly three-quarters of a century. Then, during the early summer of 1925, its career came to a sudden, rude end when a powerful earthquake shook many buildings in Santa Barbara to their foundations. When the quake struck, shortly before dawn on June 29, the keeper was asleep. But he quickly understood what was happening and herded his family outside. They reached safety just before the structure collapsed, throwing up a large cloud of masonry dust.

The old lighthouse, along with its fourth-order Fresnel lens, was completely destroyed by the quake. The station's light burned from atop a temporary wooden tower while it was being rebuilt.

One of the West's most famous lighthouse keepers was a woman. Beginning in 1865 Mrs. Julia Williams kept the Santa Barbara light for more than forty years. It is said she was away from her duties only two nights during her entire career as keeper. Her faithfulness did not keep her from raising five children, who grew up in the lighthouse.

*Rebuilt following a major earthquake, the lighthouse serves the delightful and affluent seaside resort of Santa Barbara and its well-known pier, seafood restaurants, and attractive ocean frontage.*

*The Santa Barbara Lighthouse was modest in size but well maintained before an earthquake knocked it down in 1925.* (**Courtesy National Archives**)

# POINT VICENTE LIGHT
## Los Angeles, California – 1926

### Observable

More than one keeper of the Point Vicente Lighthouse felt a chill run up and down his spine at the sight of the station's ladylike ghost. As with most lighthouse ghosts, this one was accompanied by a tragic legend. It seems the lady's lover had drowned in a shipwreck and that she walked the grounds of the light station waiting for him to rejoin her.

Unlike many other ghost stories, however, the Point Vicente apparition was not *all* talk and imagination. The keepers swore they really were seeing something, and as it turned out, their eyes had not completely deceived them. A young assistant keeper with a skeptical turn of mind began to study the lady, and before long, he had discovered her secret.

The ghost was the work of the Fresnel lens at the top of the sixty-seven-foot tower. As it rotated, the lens refracted light toward the ground in a confusion of arcs. If the refractions came together in just the right way and found a patch of fog, the "lady" appeared.

*California is a land of sharp contrasts, as the bright blue ocean, brown cliffs, and tall, white Point Vicente Lighthouse demonstrate dramatically. The lighthouse guides shipping heading for San Pedro Harbor.*

Even so, the ghostly lady still has her defenders. She remains popular with lighthouse visitors.

Built in 1926 at the edge of a cliff more than 100 feet above the Pacific, the cylindrical masonry tower is itself sixty-seven feet tall. Its extraordinarily powerful 1.1 million–candlepower light can be seen from twenty miles at sea. The light serves as a coastal marker and also helps guide ships to San Pedro Harbor.

*Point Vicente Lighthouse's lantern room glows in the dusk. The mountains of California's Channel Islands loom in the distance.*

*The Point Vicente light station is located north of Marineland off Palos Verdes Drive in Los Angeles. A drive along Hawthorne Boulevard (California 107) provides fine views of the light, which can also be seen from the Interpretive Center at 31501 Palos Verdes Drive. Near the lighthouse itself, the center offers a wealth of information about the light and the scenic Palos Verdes Peninsula. For information call (213) 377–5370.*

# POINT FERMIN LIGHT
## Los Angeles, California – 1874

Accessible

No longer functional, the Point Fermin Lighthouse remains a venerable landmark. It was built in 1874 from lumber and brick shipped around the tip of South America. Its ornate gingerbread design is unique among American lighthouses.

*A fresh coat of paint has brightened the Point Fermin Lighthouse. Built in 1874, the lighthouse is a cherished landmark and popular attraction of a Los Angeles city park.*

*Refurbished and maintained by preservationists because of its historical and architectural merit, the 1874 Point Fermin Lighthouse is the centerpiece of a Los Angeles city park. The redwood Victorian building is occupied by a park employee and is closed to the public. Located on Paseo Del Mar, west of Pacific Avenue, the park offers an excellent place to view the Los Angeles Harbor Lighthouse. For information call (213) 548–7756.*

# LOS ANGELES HARBOR LIGHT
## Los Angeles, California – 1913

Observable

As classical in appearance as its Long Beach neighbor is unconventional, the Los Angeles Harbor Lighthouse anchors the far end of the San Pedro Breakwater. Having weathered countless gales, stood through more than one earthquake, and even survived a brush with a U.S. Navy battleship, the tower leans out of plumb but remains solid and functional.

*Located at the end of the San Pedro Harbor breakwater, the Los Angeles Harbor Lighthouse rises more than seventy feet above the water.*

*Somewhat resembling a column on a Greek temple, the Los Angeles Harbor Lighthouse is located at the end of the harbor breakwater east of Pacific Avenue at Paseo Del Mar. It can be seen from Pacific Avenue and from the city park at Point Fermin, where visitors can also enjoy the Point Fermin Lighthouse.*

# OLD POINT LOMA LIGHT
## San Diego, California – 1855

### Accessible

The history of navigational markers on Point Loma runs back to Spanish times, when residents of San Diego built fires here to help royal supply ships find the harbor. Following the acquisition of California by the United States, the government undertook to erect lighthouses to help guide ships along the nation's now-lengthy western seaboard. Among these was the Old Point Loma Lighthouse, built atop the same hill where the Spanish signal fires had once burned.

Construction began in the spring of 1854 but was not completed until November of the following year. For materials, builders used locally quarried sandstone and brick brought by ship from Monterey.

The cost of the project amounted to $30,000, considerably more than had been budgeted. What was worse, once the structure was built, it quickly became apparent that Uncle Sam had not gotten all he had paid for. A first-order Fresnel lens had been ordered for the station, but when it arrived, try as they might, builders could not fit it into the lantern—the lighthouse was too small to accommodate it. Rather than tear down the building and start over, they substituted the less powerful third-order lens meant for the Humboldt Harbor Lighthouse on the northern California coast. Eventually, the big first-order lens ended up at the Cape Flattery Lighthouse, far to the north of its intended home.

Despite the smaller lens, the Point Loma Light proved very powerful indeed. Mariners could usually see it from twenty-five miles away, but some sea captains claimed to have spotted the light from a distance of nearly forty miles. The news was not all good, however. All too often clouds and fog obscured the light.

When Point Loma had been surveyed, it had seemed the perfect site for a lighthouse. Not only was it well positioned at the entrance of San Diego Harbor, it also offered an impressive elevation of more than 460 feet. This height made it the loftiest lighthouse in America but in time would also lead to its demise as an active light station. As it turned out, the elevation of the lighthouse frequently placed it above low-lying cloud banks. In heavy weather, when the light was most needed, mariners often could not see it at all.

So in 1891, thirty-six years after its lamps were first lit, the Old Point Loma Light went dark. The New Point Loma Lighthouse, built at a lower, more practical, elevation, took over its duties, and the venerable structure fell into disuse and decay. In 1913 it survived an abortive attempt to demolish it and replace it with an enormous statue of a Spanish explorer. Then, in 1933, it was rescued from ruin, renovated, and made part of the Cabrillo National Monument. As the monument's chief attraction, the lighthouse draws many thousands of visitors each year.

*The "Old" Point Loma Lighthouse is well named. It was among the first lighthouses built on America's West Coast. Construction began in 1854 and was completed the following year.*

*The iron-skeleton **Point Loma Lighthouse** replaced its more lofty ancestor in 1891. Although it could hardly be described as an architectural wonder, it continues to serve mariners today, more than a century after its construction. Its third-order Fresnel lens lights the way into San Diego Harbor.*

*The Point Loma lighthouses are the primary attractions of Cabrillo National Monument in San Diego. To reach the monument and lighthouses, follow Route 209 to the end of Point Loma. The old Cape Cod–style lighthouse, out of service since 1891, stands near the crest of the point, several hundred feet above the sea. Far below, at the edge of the Pacific, stands the iron skeleton tower that took over the work of the original lighthouse more than a century ago. Operated as a museum by the Park Service, the Old Point Loma Lighthouse is open to the public, but its hardworking neighbor is not. Yet an excellent view of the "new" Point Loma Lighthouse can be enjoyed from the road to the monument's famed tidal pools. Point Loma is a good place to watch whales during their annual southward migration in the winter. For more information on Cabrillo National Monument, call (619) 557–5450.*

# BIBLIOGRAPHY

Adams, William Henry Davenport. *Lighthouses and Lightships: A Descriptive and Historical Account of Their Mode of Construction and Organization.* New York: Scribner's, 1870.

Adamson, Hans Christian. *Keepers of the Light.* New York: Greenberg, 1955.

Beaver, Patrick. *A History of Lighthouses.* Secaucus, N.J.: Citadel, 1972.

Chase, Mary Ellen. *The Story of Lighthouses.* New York: Norton, 1965.

Holland, Francis Ross, Jr. *America's Lighthouses: Their Illustrated History Since 1716.* Brattleboro, Vt.: Stephen Greene Press, 1972.

_____*Great American Lighthouses.* Washington, D.C.: The Preservation Press, 1989.

Marx, Robert. *Shipwrecks of the Western Hemisphere.* New York: David McKay Company, 1971.

McCormick, William Henry. *The Modern Book of Lighthouses, Lifeboats, and Lightships.* London: W. Heinemann, 1913.

Moe, Christine. *Lighthouses and Lightships.* Monticello, Ill.: 1979.

Naush, John M. *Seamarks: Their History and Development.* London: Stanford Maritime, 1895.

Nelson, Sharlene and Ted. *Washington Lighthouses.* Friday Harbor, Wash.: Umbrella Books, 1990

Scheina, Robert L. "The Evolution of the Lighthouse Tower," *Lighthouses Then and Now* (supplement to the U.S. Coast Guard Commandant's Bulletin).

Snow, Edward Rowe. *Famous Lighthouses of America.* New York: Dodd, Mead, 1955.

_____*Great Gales and Disasters.* New York: Dodd, Mead, 1952.

United States Coast Guard. *Historically Famous Lighthouses.* CG-232, 1986.

West, Victor. *A Guide to Shipwreck Sites Along the Oregon Coast.* North Bend, Oreg.: West and Wells, 1984.

# ABOUT THE AUTHORS

BRUCE ROBERTS is a freelance photographer living in rural Virginia. He launched his wide-ranging career by working on newspapers in Tampa, Florida; Wilmington, Delaware; and Charlotte, North Carolina. Bruce served as director of photography and as senior photographer at *Southern Living* magazine for more than a decade. His award-winning photographs have also appeared in *Life, Sports Illustrated,* Time-Life Books, and many other magazines and books. Some of his photographs rest in the permanent collection of the Smithsonian Institution. Both the national and Georgia Nature conservancies have reprinted Bruce's nature photography.

RAY JONES began his writing career working as a reporter for weekly newspapers in Texas. He has served as an editor for Time-Life Books, as founding editor of *Albuquerque Living* magazine, and as a senior editor and writing coach at *Southern Living* magazine. Ray grew up in Macon, Georgia, where he was inspired by the writing of Hemingway and Faulkner. He is currently publisher of Country Roads Press, located in Castine, a small town on the coast of Maine.

For additional information on lighthouses and a listing of California lights
that best lend themselves to photo opportunities, contact:

Unites States Lighthouse Society
244 Kearney Street
5th Floor
San Francisco, CA 94108
(415) 362–7255


For access to lights still under Coast Guard control and not open
on a regular basis, contact:

11th Coast Guard District
400 Oceangate
Long Beach, CA 90822-5399
(310) 980–4300, ext. 144

Public Affairs Detachment (11 District North)
Coast Guard Building 42
Alameda, CA 94501-5100
(510) 437–3318

13th Coast Guard District
915 2nd Avenue
Seattle, WA 98174-1067
(206) 553–5896